PRE-1841 CENSUSES & POPULATION LISTINGS

IN THE BRITISH ISLES

Colin R Chapman

D0861259

FIFTH EDITION

First Edition 1990
Second (revised) Edition 1991
Third (revised) Edition 1992
Fourth Edition 1994
Fifth Edition 1998
All editions published as part of the
Chapmans Records Cameos series by
Lochin Publishing, 6 Holywell Road, Dursley,
Gloucestershire GL11 5RS, England

Fifth Edition published in the U.S.A. by
Genealogical Publishing Co., Inc.
1001 N. Calvert St., Baltimore, MD 21202
Second printing 2004

Library of Congress Catalogue Card Number 99-71501
International Standard Book Number 0-8063-1613-6
Made in the United States of America

The cover illustration is adapted by Sarah Elliott from
P. Brueghel's "The Numbering at Bethlehem" - one of the
earliest pre-1841 censuses - mentioned in the Preface.

---

*Titles in the Chapmans Records
Cameos series:*

Tracing Your British Ancestors

The Growth of British Education & Its Records

Ecclesiastical Courts, Their Officials and Their Records

Marriage Laws, Rites and Customs

Weights, Money & Other Measures Used by Our Ancestors

Some Central & Eastern European Ancestry

Table of Contents

Abbreviations & Addresses

BL	British Library, 96 Euston Road, London, NW1 2DB.
FFHS	Federation of Family History Societies, Benson Room, Birmingham & Midland Institute, Margaret Street, Birmingham B3 3BS.
	FFHS Publications Ltd, 2-4 Killer Street, Ramsbottom, Bury, Lancs, BL0 9BZ.
INA	Irish National Archives, Bishop Street, Dublin 2.
NAS	National Archives of Scotland, HM General Register House, Princes Street, Edinburgh, EH1 3YY.
NLI	National Library of Ireland, Kildare Street, Dublin 2.
NLW	National Library of Wales, Penglais, Aberystwyth, Dyfed, SY23 3BU.
PRO	Public Record Office, Ruskin Avenue, Kew, TW9 4DU.
PRONI	Public Record Office of Northern Ireland, 66 Balmoral Avenue, Belfast, BT9 6NY.
RCB	Representative Church Body, Braemore Park, Rathgar, Dublin 14.
SoG	Society of Genealogists, 14 Charterhouse Buildings, Goswell Road, London, EC1M 7BA.

Preface

The continuing demands for copies of this Cameo have offered an opportunity to revise the text and appendices and incorporate over 200 additional listings for Ireland in this fifth and yet larger edition. I can, therefore, offer this as a unique chronological account of censuses and enumerations in the British Isles from 1086 to 1841. For those studying Irish social and family history, census listings can fill in so many gaps created by the loss of other historical documents. Reviewers now appear to recognise that I have examined and described material well beyond the bounds of the eighteenth century, although it should be appreciated that the frequency of undertaking censuses and surveys, all around the country, did increase significantly following Potter's Bill of 1753. There are over 100 national taxes and other allied listings in the Index, but do consult Appendix I and then the appropriate year in the text to local scores of other censuses resulting from local initiatives.

In 1973 the Bedfordshire Historical Record Society published a transcript of the 1782 census of Cardington, edited by David Baker. In my student days in chemical research I had been taught to pursue information indicated in bibliographies and to follow up and read references in full. It was reading the works quoted by Baker that inspired me to locate other similar censuses, enumerations, surveys and lists of people. Thus the journey on my quest began, fitted in around my many other commitments at that time, not the least of which were my periods of office within the Federation of Family History Societies. I was able to reach the initial public milestone in my quest at the First British Family History Conference in 1980, appropriately at Bedford, when I gave a lecture on pre-1841 censuses - incorporating the Cardington census into my presentation. In my audience was Jeremy S W Gibson (JSWG, as I have referred to him in the ensuing pages) who immediately suggested I commit that lecture to paper for broader consumption.

At that time my diverse responsibilities did not permit my doing so; but I have been pleased to note that JSWG took up the challenge himself and personally followed many of the examples I quoted. With his unique enthusiasm he contacted or visited the various record offices around the British Isles for details of their holdings, culminating in not a few of the Gibson Guides, published by the Federation of Family History Societies. To JSWG I am, accordingly, grateful for drawing some early population listings to the attention of a wider audience than I or Baker, my guru *in absentio*, had originally considered.

Over the intervening years, however, I have acceded to many requests to deliver lectures on this topic to audiences all over the world. And during the period several individuals, many of them now firm friends, have planted further milestones in my quest by providing me with more lists of people prior to 1841. On very many occasions members of my audiences have repeated JSWG's original suggestion that I make my notes available in a more permanent format. It is in response to these requests that another milestone was reached when I prepared the first edition of this Cameo in 1990. I was delighted that its publication inspired others to dig into national and local archives and ferret out other lists which I incorporated into my previous editions in 1991, 1992 and 1994. Very many correspondents including several archivists, excited after reading those earlier editions, have informed me of nineteenth century returns they sought and found; so many, in fact, that I must add their findings to this edition before my pending tray crashes through the study floor into the basement.

With my 1980 lecture as the framework and the numerous additional examples acquired over two decades I have compiled the following account. I have been terribly unacademic and have unashamedly interwoven simple enumerations of people, even surveys and numbers of houses, with detailed listings which furnish names, ages, addresses, occupations, religious affiliations and more. Local unique lists are jumbled among national surveys, military with peaceful, and the ecclesiastical and civil are side by side. I have even tossed in a few taxation lists which affected only a small proportion of the community as I consider such lists are very much under-utilised as sources of names. My critics may protest; but I firmly believe that serious family historians will need to set their ancestors into the total context of the local, county and national situation. Hence even numbers can provide that additional gem to the polished family history. Whilst casual name collectors or pedigree producers may, therefore, find the following pages rather irritating, even they may discover some of the references useful in their specific searches. And here I must express particular thanks to the librarians of the University Libraries at Bristol and Birmingham and of the Royal Society of Chemistry, who have permitted me to spend many happy hours dipping into periodicals, stretching back over 200 years, to locate references to early population listings. The staff of the British Library, especially when it was housed within the British Museum, were equally patient in assisting me to understand the logic of their nineteenth century cataloguers. At the Guildhall Library, London, the staff have helped to locate some nineteenth century censuses of the City parishes. It is in tribute to these librarians that I have provided for readers of this Cameo, who have similar curiosity to my own, detailed references - many scores of them - should they wish to read the original accounts.

There are regular articles on, and references to, censuses and enumerations in specialist journals such as *Population Studies, Local Population Studies,* and publications of the Cambridge Group for the History of Population and Social Structure, a unit of the Social Science Research Council. Each of these has assisted me in seeking examples of listings of one sort or another, and with their continued publication will undoubtedly provide further examples as they come to light.

I have followed a chronological sequence - after all that is how we enjoy our lives - rather than use a geographical or thematic ordering of events; indeed many a census was taken as a consequence of the success or failure of a preceding one, and to hop otherwise than in a successive pattern would lead to certain confusion. Thus to appease those who have not the patience or determination to examine every page of my text I have, in addition to the Index, appended (in Appendix I) a county-by-county breakdown of the various censuses containing individuals' names with the dates of those censuses. I have expanded on many of the listings within the main text of this Cameo. For completeness I have also appended (in Appendix II), but with little comment, a list of decennial censuses containing names of individuals from 1801 to 1831. Where a return with names for a particular parish has not yet been discovered for those years, but one taken for whatever purpose in a nearby year is known, I have included it in Appendix II. Again the purists may protest, but I believe that those anxious for names will be grateful.

In my text I have failed to distinguish between enumerations which were *de jure* and those which were *de facto* - the former requiring people to return to their places of origin to be counted (as at the Nativity of Christ i.e. the *Numbering at Bethlehem* illustrated on the cover of this Cameo), and the latter requiring the survey to be taken of the contemporary population in a particular place (the more common situation, as exemplified during the nineteenth and twentieth centuries). But I assume that such distinctions will be of little concern to the majority of my readers. In general I have arbitrarily reserved the term census to indicate a listing where names of people are included; and where only numbers are provided I have used the term enumeration. But I have occasionally lapsed from my own definitions in my enthusiasm to encourage researchers to consult original documents. Hopefully those who know me will be understandingly patronising in this regard.

I am aware that many local listings may exist further to those I have quoted on the following pages. In this Cameo I have concentrated on providing examples of population listings within the British Isles which may be of value in historical research, or even of passing interest to the curious. Accordingly, I would be delighted to be informed of other local listings, together with any notes on their original purposes, their present whereabouts or availability of copies which could be consulted by fellow researchers.

A complementary publication by Mervyn Medlycott, in association with Jeremy Gibson, is available. It provides fuller lists of local census listings than in my appendices - but not their detailed backgrounds as I have described here.

COLIN R CHAPMAN.

1. 1841 - The Ultimate Census

1841 is regarded by many who are interested in British genealogical research as the beginning of an era - the first of the nineteenth century returns of use to the family historian. Names and occupations are quoted and ages given to the nearest five years (rounded downwards); the birthplace is stated as being within or outside the county of residence. Equally important, individuals are grouped together in households, each householder having filled in, probably with assistance, a separate schedule.

In reality, however, the 1841 census is more of an end product, the acme of campaigning and correspondence which had been pursued for decades, even generations. A major victory was achieved in 1800 when the principle of a national enumeration of the people was accepted, in the *Population Act*, by the parliament of that time. Many attempts had been made before the nineteenth century to persuade English monarchs and governments, and even the Church, to conduct a national census; Bills had been introduced into and laid before parliaments, but all had failed either because of lack of time to debate the argument, lack of finance to implement the aspirations or a total lack of support for the proposed legislation.

Even when the national, decennial census was introduced in England and Wales and in Scotland and the Channel Islands in 1801, the authorities neither requested nor required the names of individuals; the only information solicited was the number of males and females employed in agriculture; the number employed in trade, manufactures or handicraft; and the number not in either of these two categories. Although this system provided enumerations a certain amount of confusion arose as many women and children and servants were put into the third category, irrespective of their actual occupations. In an attempt to resolve these anomalies the 1811 and 1821 questionnaires requested the number of families in each category, and the results were published as numerical analyses by counties, hundreds, parishes, and townships or municipal boroughs. The actual texts of the Population Acts from 1800 to 1830 referred to the various names used in different parts of the country to describe administrative divisions; namely: stewartry, division, rape, wapentake, lathe, precinct, soke, franchise, liberty, city, borough, town or county corporate in which a parish, township or place could be situated. It may be noted here that the taking of a census every ten years did not begin on the Isle of Man until 1811 and in Ireland until 1821 (see below), in contrast to 1801 for the remainder of the British Isles.

The employment categories were extended from three to seven in 1831 and the category of trade and handicraft was further divided into specific occupations; these had to be indicated on the formula (as a specific form was called at that time) compiled by the local constable or overseer who conducted the enumeration. 1821 was the only occasion prior to 1841 when an age structure (albeit a crude one) was requested; and whilst in 1801 the numbers of inhabited and uninhabited houses were required, as in all subsequent censuses, the number of houses being built was not included as a question until 1811.

The *Population Act* of 1800 further required every incumbent to supply the numbers of baptisms and burials in his parish for both males and females from 1700 to 1780 and also for each year from 1781 to 1800; the number of marriages in each year from 1754 to 1800 was also required. The printed summaries of the enumerations published by central government, which are certainly worthy of study, include these parochial statistics by counties and hundreds and for the larger cities. In 1811, 1821, 1831 similar questions on vital statistics for the preceding ten years were asked, and in 1831 information on the ages of deceased persons from 1813 to 1830 and the number of illegitimate births was requested as well. Again, the printed summaries provide the numerical analyses of the results submitted.

Whilst the 1800 Act elicited only numbers of people, and the printed summaries contain the same data in an organised format, many enumerators made detailed listings of their local populations and included names, family groups and relationships, ages, even dates of birth, and added notes of immigration patterns into their parishes. Some early nineteenth century censuses thus provide similar, or greater, information than that available in the 1841 or even the 1851 returns. Prior to 1841, however, this information was not required by the authorities collating the data centrally and so it was not normally forwarded to London; consequently these detailed censuses, where they survive, are in a variety of locations. Some appear in parish registers of baptisms, marriages or burials, often on the inside of the front or back cover. Some returns appear in the account books of the overseers of the poor for a particular parish. Some are found within the churchwardens' accounts books. Some of these early nineteenth century census returns were recorded in notebooks used specifically for that purpose and are to be found in the parish chest with other parochial documents.

Some of these records have found their way into county record offices; others into museums, into local reference libraries, or into borough archives. Others remained among the personal papers of the schoolmaster, overseer, churchwarden, or incumbent who conducted the census survey - and have gone the way of all such private papers: a few have survived and have been deposited in suitable archive offices; some are possibly retained even now in private hands; but the majority have perished, their value unrecognized by the custodians of such documents. In the first editions of this Cameo, it was stated that these nineteenth century returns were being discovered slowly. But this very publication has catalyzed the search for similar returns and very many others have been brought to light in recent years and drawn to the attention of the author and his publishers. It is hoped that yet more will be discovered, their presence recorded, and their content transcribed, indexed and published.

In Ireland, regular national censuses began only in 1821, but recorded far more details than were requested elsewhere in the British Isles. The Irish returns for 1821 and 1831 have the names, ages and occupations of everyone and their relationship to the head of the household. In 1821 even the number of storeys in their homes was noted, and in 1831 their religion was recorded. These pre-1841 censuses for Ireland are, therefore, considerably more valuable to researchers than those for most of the British Isles. Unfortunately many originals were destroyed in 1922, although a significant number of extracts (now in the Irish National Archives - INA) had been made by Gertrude Thrift, and some returns with names of individuals have survived for at least parts of most counties (see Appendix II). The surviving 1831 census for Dublin St Bride's appears to be a copy as it shows only the names and religion of the heads of households and the numbers and religions of the other adults and children in the household.

Many 1801, 1811, 1821 and 1831 censuses, including those for Ireland, which list individuals by name and give other details are quoted in Appendix II. After 1831 the organisation for conducting the censuses was greatly improved. The 1836 *Registration Act*, which introduced civil registration with local registrars responsible through Superintendent Registrars to the Registrar General, identified more reliable individuals who could be called upon to administer the censuses as well as a framework through which subsequent censuses could be managed.

Prior to the nineteenth century, lists of names of people had been compiled by the State, by Lords of Manors and by the Church (and occasionally by others for curiosity or reasons unclear to us today). The State was interested in potential tax payers from whom a financial duty, levy, tax, subsidy or relief (the description varied over the years) could be extracted to develop the nation's infrastructure, improve facilities, provide a welfare system or, from time to time, fight an adversary (usually the French, Dutch or Spanish). To facilitate military recruitment, other lists were drawn up of men capable of bearing arms or fit to fight in the regular or territorial forces: hence Muster Rolls and Militia Lists were compiled. The lists drawn up by Lords of Manors were for very similar purposes.

The Church needed to fund its evangelising and pastoral activities and to identify its supporters and defaulters. Before the Reformation the Church in the British Isles was Roman Catholic; but from the sixteenth century the Established (Anglican) Protestant Church emerged, and non-conforming Christians were generally Catholic or Puritan. Such dissidents were also regarded as potential opponents of the Crown as the Sovereign assumed the mantle of titular head of the Church of England. Accordingly, the Church made lists of loyal Protestant adherents and communicants, and of overt oponents and even potential trouble-makers such as "Popish People", Papists and Roman Catholics in general. Whatever are our thoughts today on the ethics of these actions, the lists of names of people that were generated are extremely useful in historical research.

The Church, after being embraced by the Sovereign, never questioned its right to impose a tax on the Sovereign's subjects - in other words on every possible tax-payer such as a land owner or householder, even an occupier or tenant. Hence, traditionally, all landowners in England, Wales and Ireland were compelled to pay tithes in kind towards the finances of the Established (Anglican) Church. This was resented by many non-Anglicans. These payments in kind were abolished in favour of a monetary payment in Ireland by the 1823 *Composition Act*, and in England and Wales by the 1836 *Tithe Commutation Act*; land valuations obviously had to be undertaken to determine the amounts payable as a result of these Acts. The associated valuation lists and schedules for England, Wales and Ireland are fully discussed in the Cameo *Tracing Your British Ancestors*. However, the Irish valuations, recorded in Tithe Applotment Books between 1823 and 1838, generated lists of names of landowners by townlands and baronies (similar in sizes to parishes and hundreds); these offer replacements, however less detailed, for the nineteenth century census returns missing for Ireland. Another listing, the Primary Valuation of Ireland, known as Griffith's Valuation (after the Land Commissioner, Richard Griffith), is beyond the scope of this Cameo, being published between 1848 and 1864 as a basis for local taxation. However, it is worth noting that the names of persons in both the 1820's Tithe Applotment Books and Griffith's Valuation have been indexed, county by county, by the National Library of Ireland (NLI) in the Householders' Index, sometimes referred to as the Index of Surnames. Another useful, but with a misleading title, series of listings of names in Ireland are the Marksmen Lists of 1837; nothing to do with skillful archers, these were the lists of persons entitled to vote but who could make only a mark, not sign their names. For mostly parliamentary boroughs in counties from Antrim to Westmeath, these lists were published in *Parliamentary Papers* for 1837 in Appendix A of Vol 11 (I) as Reports from Committees.

2. Listings to 1629

Although the 1800 *Population Act* initiated the holding of decennial censuses from 1801, which became more sophisticated as they developed through the nineteenth century, censuses had been taken long before this time, both in the British Isles as well as further afield. Enumerations were even more common, the numbering of the Children of Israel in 1200 BC being one of the earliest documented [1]. There is ample evidence that the Romans conducted a census every five or fourteen years; a good example is that of 5 BC. The one held by Governor Cyrenius in AD 6 almost led to open revolt as those involved objected to the prospect of being called into military service. However, such enumerations rarely included names of individuals; and although population numbers are of use to demographers and statisticians, alone they are of lesser value to the family historian. On the other hand, population statistics for a community in which named ancestors can be identified are a most useful source of data through which individuals can be visualised and depicted in their contemporary context.

One of the first censuses in the British Isles of which we have tangible evidence was the Domesday Survey of 1086. This was compiled by Norman clerks at the instruction of William I, who wanted to know the extent of the land he had conquered and how it was managed. Landholders were listed by name and an indication was given of their status - villein, bordar, or serf [2]. At this time land-holders were generally male, thus the Domesday census provides listings mostly of adult males.

From this date throughout the country very many returns were made of individuals for various purposes and by various authorities. A glance at the Index to this Cameo gives an indication of the range of returns available. Both Church and State, which in some eras were inseparable and almost indistinguishable (even if in other eras their policies were totally polarised), conducted surveys of the people, often for the purpose of raising revenue. Some surveys were locally organised and for specific areas, while others were implemented nationally. The originals of many of these early surveys are held in the Public Record Office (PRO); not a few have been transcribed, translated and published by historical record societies and antiquarian or archaeological societies beginning late in the nineteenth century [3].

In 1181 a Saladin Tithe (sometimes referred to as a Moveables Tax) was imposed on individuals' personalty - in contrast to their real estate. As the rate was calculated on one-tenth of the value of the possessions for urban dwellers and one-fifteenth for rural dwellers, this duty was also termed the One-tenth and One-fifteenth Tax by some authorities. In some parts of the country the actual value of the goods being assessed was declared and sworn as correct by the owners, in other areas jurors made the assessments. This tax remained on the statute books until 1623 although it was not enforced much after the medieval period.

From 1194 until 1224 the method of raising revenue reverted to assessments of real estate and a Hideage, Hidegeld or Carucage Tax was levied on each hide (or carucate) of land held. The division of land was based on the Domesday survey taken in the previous century.

Freemen's Rolls or Registers, such as those for the City of York from 1272, were maintained by Corporate Towns as a record of the names of freemen and guild members. Normally freemen were able to claim certain privileges in their borough or city, such as shares in the town's profits and exemption from tolls. Some of these registers have been transcribed and published by historical record societies, such as the *Register of the Freemen of the City of York, Volume I, 1272-1558* edited by Dr Francis Collins for the Surtees Society [4].

The *Statute of Winchester* (1285) required every man between 15 and 60 to be assessed and sworn to arms according to his land and chattels (i.e. his real estate and his personalty). The view of arms was to be made twice a year in each hundred and liberty by two constables; and when the justices visited the district the constables were to present any defaulters. This was not innovative but up-dated the Anglo Saxon idea of a Fyrd (army) which had been developed by King Alfred to enable all men between 15 and 60 to serve their shire when called upon to do so; the motive was to prevent a repetition of the Danish invasion and so all possible fit and capable men were identified so they could be called away from their normal activities to help defend their locality. In reality calling men away from their places of work was likely to disrupt the local community and the local economy; thus the lists drawn up were likely to contain not all those between 15 and 60 capable of bearing arms, but those who could be spared locally. Thus any lists resulting from the Statute were by no means true censuses, and whilst at least two lists should have been made annually for each area, few appear to have survived. The Sussex listing in 1297 of ninety Gentlemen who were summoned to London for military service would seem to be a direct result of the 1285 Statute.

Between 1290 and 1332 sixteen [5] grants or subsidies were levied by the monarchs as methods of raising revenue. These were not annual taxes but were imposed as the need arose; accordingly, each subsidy was governed by the conditions laid down in the Act by which it was implemented. The normal rate of assessment was four shillings in the pound per annum on land worth twenty shillings and upwards, and two shillings and eight pence in the pound per annum on personal possessions worth three pounds and upwards. One, two or three subsidies might be granted by the same Act to bring in the necessary revenue, and payment could be spread over a year or more. The returns of those liable to pay were inscribed on parchment rolls and so commonly called Lay Subsidy Rolls. Unfortunately no British county has a complete set of these rolls, and there were many individuals who evaded payment whose names are thus unrecorded.

A further forty-two grants were levied between 1334 and 1434; but for these the wealth of each vill was assessed, so employing a different system from that of the earlier lay subsidies which used the wealth of individuals as the basis for the taxation. Thus the fourteenth century returns normally show the quotas for the villages only and do not name individuals. However, for Cornwall, Devon, Kent and Sussex, names are given. These lists provide a useful source of English sur-names. The originals of these grants are held in the PRO [6].

In 1377, 1379 and 1381 England suffered some crises as a result of wars, so further taxes were levied on all males over the age of fourteen. The taxpayers' names were recorded on poll tax lists for those years. Like the former lists, these are not true censuses since females and those under the age of fourteen are obviously missing and there were several evasions; but the names of those who did pay were recorded - normally in Latin, although those for Northumberland were in French. There was less evasion in 1377, when a flat rate of a groat per person was levied; this year is particularly useful to family historians for London, Carlisle, Colchester, Hull and Oxford. In 1379 and 1381 the rate was graded socially and the receipts, where they survive, contain the names of taxpayers and the amounts paid.

The 1488 list of resident males of Rye [7], Sussex, eligible to serve as constable or watchout for the town is one of the earliest local lists of names - but 1523 marks the year for the first census (in a form resembling that used in the nineteenth century) which has so far been discovered for anywhere in the British Isles. Part of the city of Coventry (ten wards) [8] was surveyed and a listing compiled of its inhabitants. The original census is held in Coventry by the city archivist.

The pretext of a muster to arms by counties and hundreds (see the 1285 *Statute of Winchester*) was used in 1522 to undertake a nation-wide valuation of properties. Some of the resultant Muster Lists and Rolls for several counties for this year have found their way into the Exchequer series of documents at the PRO [9] , which has produced one of its Records Information Leaflets - number 46 - on Militia Muster Lists and Rolls 1522-1640. Holdings, by counties, for these and subsequent muster and militia lists are detailed in *Tudor and Stuart Muster Rolls*, produced by Alan Dell and Jeremy Gibson; this booklet was republished in 1991 by the Federation of Family History Societies (FFHS). Detailed commentaries on the militia from 1558 were published by Routledge and Kegan Paul in 1965 and 1967 [10]. Lists for 1535 and 1536, for 1539 and 1540, for 1542 and for 1569 survive for many counties, either at the PRO, the British Library (BL), the Bodleian Library or county record offices, as detailed by Dell and Gibson.

In 1524 and 1525 lay subsidies, further to those of the late fourteenth century, were imposed on a national basis and on top of the previous one tenth and one fifteenth taxes (the so-called Saladin Tithe or Moveables Tax, first imposed in 1181). During the period 1524-25 the methods of taxation were based on three alternative assessments of the taxpayers' capacity: the capital value of property, landed income, and wages. The value of these particular lay subsidies was emphasised by Dr Maurice Beresford [11] who stated "The assessment rolls, where they survive, provide a directory of the upper, middle and lower-middle classes and are near enough to earliest parish registers (1538) to serve as some basis for genealogical tree planting".

A list of families in the archdeaconry of Stafford was compiled in 1532. Although not a complete census in that not all inhabitants were listed, it provides some fifty-one thousand names arranged in family groups and states the surname of the head of the family, his Christian name, and the names of his wife and children. The list is unusual because former (deceased) wives and dead children are also included. Its original purpose is uncertain, but it was possibly a list of those entitled to prayers in return for some contribution to church fabric maintenance. As this listing also pertains to the pre-parish register era, its value to British family history for the Stafford locality is immense. An edited and indexed transcription was published in 1976 [12] by the Staffordshire Record Society.

Information on the population of Wales from 1536 to 1801 (or, to be more accurate, the paucity of such information) was discussed in 1937 by David Williams in the *Bulletin of the Board of Celtic Studies* [13], published in Cardiff by the Press Board of the University of Wales.

In 1545 a listing of the population of Kidlington in Oxfordshire was made, thus providing some useful information, particularly as the parish registers there do not commence until 1574. 1545 was an eventful year for Kidlington for in that year the Duke of Suffolk died so that the Manor passed into private hands (those of John Blundell and Leonard Chamberlayne); Henry Lawrence also died, bequeathing his books to Exeter College, Oxford - he was the last Roman Catholic vicar for the parish remaining from prior to the King's break with Rome.

The fascinating Sheep Tax, introduced in March 1549, was debated in some detail by Beresford in the first and second issues of the *Agricultural History Review* [14] which began as a regular publication of the British Agricultural Historical Society in 1953. The national requirement to tax all flocks of sheep and accordingly to list their size and owners by counties appears to have failed and the relief, as it was termed, was discontinued in January 1550. Nevertheless the returns for Hunting-donshire, now in the PRO, are very good and those for Yorkshire, listed by Ridings, merit study as do those for Devon, and the counties of Nottingham and Oxford. In a number of cases the names and addresses of flock owners living out of the county (possibly the first example of "strays") are given. Such information is valuable in the preparation of a rural social or family history.

On the Statute Books, also for 1549, there is mention of a national Cloth Tax as another means of raising revenue. However, the returns for this relief do not appear to have survived and it is uncertain if it was ever enforced or even imposed.

After taking the Church in Britain from Rome, Henry VIII retained the practice of parishes levying an annual tithe on all parishioners at Easter; from part of this tithe, incumbents derived an income. Lists of parishioners were made in the so-called Easter Books or Pascal Rolls, several of which have survived for some English and two Welsh-border counties, Flint and Monmouth. Even one pre-Reformation book for Hornsea, Yorkshire, for Easter 1450, has been found and that for Oundle, Northamptonshire continues until 1869 (though with other details and starting very much later); but for some counties and for Scotland and Ireland, none has been located. Some helpful articles by Sue Wright on Easter Books were published in 1985 and 1989 [15].

The 1551 Parliamentary Act for the *Provision and Relief of the Poor* required parish lists to be compiled of persons potentially in need of assistance. None appears to have survived for this year but others are extant: Norwich for 1570, Warwick for 1587, Ipswich for 1597 and Salisbury for 1635. These lists are useful and unusual as they portray a relatively large number of people at the bottom of the social ladder. As a consequence such listings are sometimes referred to as a "Poor Census". They contain names of individuals, their ages, addresses and occupations and in some cases the parishes of their long-time residences or births. The Norwich listing also includes those who were contributing towards the poor rate and identifies master craftsmen and others who had undertaken an apprenticeship but who had temporarily failed; this is apparent as some of the individuals later apprenticed their sons to other craftsmen. The original of this census is held at Norfolk Record Office although an annotated transcription with a descriptive commentary was edited by John F Pound and published by the Norfolk Record Society [16] in 1971. The Ipswich listing was published by the Suffolk Record Society in July 1966.

Freemen's Rolls or Registers have already been mentioned (see 1272), and for the City of York another series began in 1559. These, continued until 1759 in a second volume, were also transcribed, edited by Dr Collins and published by the Surtees Society in the late nineteenth century. Towards the end of the twentieth century the York Freemen records were re-examined by John Malden; his work is more comprehensive and, having indexes available on microfiche to Freemen, Apprentices and Masters, is even more useful [17]. Similar listings were prepared for London and other corporate towns, and in many cases these have also been published.

The 1563 Ecclesiastical Return of Families, which laid down the number of families in every diocese in England, may prove of some value to the family historian; with a suitable multiplier (4.25 is the accepted figure for this return) one can compute the total population for a particular area. Thus a family can be set in the local or the national population context even though the names of individuals are not quoted in the returns. The originals of this return, conducted diocese by diocese, are held among the Harleian Manuscripts [18] in the British Library.

A schedule of the inhabitants of some Canterbury parishes was compiled around 1565. This contains not only the names of the householders, their wives and the numbers of their children (and in some instances also their names and ages), but also the numbers of their servants. Furthermore, this census must be unique as it also contains the numbers of dogs and hogs kept by each householder. This schedule is deposited at the Kent County Archives Office in Maidstone [19].

The Communicants' Lists for Canterbury Diocese in 1565, also deposited at Maidstone [19], are very descriptive for some parishes, especially Eythorne and Waldershare, and amount to almost complete censuses.

A cerificate of 27 May 1571, portraying the names of all strangers resident and abiding within the port and town of Sandwich, Kent, was deposited with the State Papers, held now at the PRO. This listing [20] identifies how many of the strangers were denizens and what was the nation of their origin.

On 5 May 1574 a survey was conducted in Poole, Dorset, by Robert Nicholas and Denis Howse, who were constables of the town. In general each householder only is named and there is mention of "his wife" and the numbers of his sons, daughters and servants, although some servants' names are given. Ages or addresses are not generally stated, although those living in the almshouses in two named streets are identified. Also in the document, but taken on 16 July that year, is a list of ships and ship-owners, obviously in Poole harbour, which gives the names of the master and the seafaring men, as well as the name of each vessel and her owner. Included in this census is a note of the names of those who are to attend and serve at the Castle of Brownsea. The original survey is with the borough archives at Poole, but photocopies are available in Dorset Record Office and Poole Reference Library.

Initiated by a Statute of 1581 and by later statutes, lists were compiled on a national basis from 1582 to 1682, at irregular intervals, of those who absented themselves from divine service at the (Established) parish church. These recusants lists or rolls, now held in the PRO [21], are the annual returns to the Exchequer of the fines and forfeitures imposed; thus they do not contain the names of all the recusants of that time, only those who were compelled to pay. In many cases the recusant's religious denomination is stated. Some of the lists of recusants appear to have been copied contemporarily, probably for the benefit of the diocesan authorities; such copies have found their way into a variety of archives, some now being at the BL, some at the House of Lords Record Office, some at the Bodleian Library in Oxford and some are in county record offices. Several of the lists have been transcribed, a selection of which has been published by the Catholic Record Society [22].

At Courteenhall in Northamptonshire, in about 1587, the rector made a list of the parish inhabitants by families with the dates of their births or baptisms. The earliest date on the document is 31 December 1538. This Incumbent's Visiting List was added to over subsequent years and developed into a series of pedigree charts, the last addition being made on 28 January 1617. The document was at some later date bound into the first parish register for Courteenhall, and is now in the county archives [23] in Northampton.

1590 is an example of a year that might have become the genealogists' fulcrum, not because of a census as such but the potential for everybody's name being recorded on a national basis. Lord Burghley, Lord Treasurer at the time, sent a proposal to the Archbishop of Canterbury for the establishment of a General Register Office. Unfortunately over 200 years had to pass before such a proposal fell on sympathetic ears.

The original of the Caernarvonshire Subsidy Roll for 1597/8 is typical of a census in this form which has been deposited in the PRO [24]. The list of names was transcribed, edited and published in 1937 with a commentary by Emyr Gwynne Jones in the *Bulletin of the Board of Celtic Studies* [25].

In 1599 Richard Phillips (constable) and William Gurnall (headborough) conducted a census of Ealing, Middlesex and included the names, occupations and ages of the inhabitants. The original material is held in the PRO [26] but a transcript was published by Ealing Local History Society in 1962. This provides a most valuable list at the end of the sixteenth century of the inhabitants of a Middlesex village now swallowed up as a suburb of Greater London.

Two censuses were conducted in the borough of Marlborough, Wiltshire in 1600 and 1601. The first, in June 1600, is a list of those in the borough who contributed financially towards the purchase of armour or armoury for the fight against Spain. It was accordingly known locally as a levy towards "Armour for the Armada". The 1601 census was conducted to ascertain the names of those men in the borough who were between the ages of 17 and 60, and was thus a militia muster listing (see 1522) rather than a true census. Men in this age range were considered capable of bearing arms, and so fit to fight, presumably against the Spaniards; taking this and the subscription raised the previous year into account there must have been some considerable anti-Iberian feeling in Marlborough, at least, at this period.

Manorial surveys were conducted in many parts of the country from around the year 1600. The ownerships of tenements were traced back to their owner "*ex antiquo*", which in practice amounted from about sixty to seventy years. Such surveys provide surnames retaining the same tenements and thus a history of the tenancies. For example at Barton-le-Cley, Bedfordshire, a house with eighteen acres which was occupied by John Foster in 1603 was previously occupied by Thomas Rudd, who had taken it over from John Rudd, who had taken it over from Richard Ellis in 1551, who had taken it over from a Mr Burnard in 1512. It is interesting to note in this case that by 1671 only the Foster surname was still extant in the parish. The decline (or increase) in the fortunes of a family can also be traced through a study of these surveys by noting the amounts paid, or even exemptions permitted, for successive years.

Another national enumeration for ecclesiastical purposes, similar to the 1563 census, was made in 1603, but this time the numbers of communicants in each parish were noted. Some of these communicants' lists are in the British Library [27], some in county record offices, and others in diocesan record offices (mostly given to the care of the county archivist today). Many of the 1603 lists have been transcribed and published [28].

In 1608 a census was taken of men in Gloucestershire. This described their occupations and indicated the distribution of industries in the county. The original return is in the county archives but an analysis and commentary [29] on the census was published in the *Economic History Review* in 1934.

In the Irish counties of Cavan, Donegal and Fermanagh, several Scottish and English undertakers (landlords) were granted land in 1612-13. The names of the grantees, which comprise one of the earliest census-type listings for Ireland, were published by the Historical Manuscripts Commission in 1947 [30].

The total population of Guernsey in 1615 has been estimated in several histories of the island, for example Ansted and Latham's work on the Channel Islands in 1862. A commentary by G H Dury on the Guernsey figures was published [31] in the quarterly journal of the Geographical Association in 1948.

At irregular intervals between 1615 and 1628 detailed lists of the inhabitants of the village of Cogenhoe, Northamptonshire, were compiled by Christopher Spicer, the rector, and included in his parish registers. In some years he listed the individuals alphabetically by Christian names, in other years alphabetically by family surname, and other years apparently arbitrarily. For those who have ancestors in that tiny community these lists would prove a fascinating study even though it is by no means a true census. The parish register [32] containing the original surveys is in the county record office in Northampton.

In 1622 a census was undertaken of the inhabitants of the borough of Stafford. A commentary on this census was written by Ruth M Kidson and published in the *Transactions of the Old Stafford Society* for 1956-59. The original returns [33] are in the county record office at Stafford.

3. Seventeenth century listings: 1630 to 1699

The Irish Muster Rolls for 1630 list names of the larger landlords in Ulster and the able-bodied men they could assemble if needed. A complete copy, arranged by counties and districts, is in Armagh County Library; copies are in the National Library of Ireland (NLI) and the Public Record Office of Northern Ireland (PRONI).

A list of the Vills and Freeholders of Derbyshire was made in 1633, although the original purpose of the list is uncertain. What appeared to be a draft manuscript of this listing was held privately (by G A Cubley of Sheffield) in 1884, but is now lost. Fortunately, however, it was transcribed by Sidney Oldall Addy who published the names of the vills and the individual freeholders in the annual volume [34] of the Derbyshire Archaeological and Natural History Society for that year.

A survey of the inhabitants of the City of London was undertaken in 1638 as a result of an order of the King in Council dated 22 April 1638. The clergy of London were required to make an estimate of the rental value of the houses in each of the 107 City parishes together with the actual tithe paid for each house. The original returns, which are now in Lambeth Palace Library, for 93 of the City parishes contain the names of householders, the rentals paid for the houses and the tithes paid. Some incumbents described the locations of the houses in their parishes in great detail, others did not even state the Christian names of the householders; thus the information for each parish varies enormously. Nevertheless an edited, but usefully indexed, transcription of this return was published in 1931 by the Society of Genealogists (SoG).

Another list of the City of London, but this time of the "Principal Inhabitants" was made in 1640, by wards. The returns, nowadays held in the PRO, list those inhabitants in each ward who were prepared to assist Charles I by offering financial security; the wards were arranged alphabetically, but there are no inhabitants for some wards on the list. A copy of the list was made and published in 1886 "from original returns in the Public Record Office made by the Aldermen of the several wards of the City of London, naming such Inhabitants as were conceived able to lend the King (Charles I) money upon security raising £200,000, according to order of the Privy Council, dated 10 May 1640". The list was republished more usefully by Pinhorns in 1969 who added an index of the names compiled by C F H Evans.

Surveys of land ownership in Ireland were compiled in 1640 (Books of Survey and Distribution), and by Sir William Petty in 1654-56 (The Civil Survey) and 1659 (Pender's Census), prior to re-allocation of land by the English government. To substantiate the information, details from deeds and wills were included in the 1654-56 survey, published by The Irish Manuscripts Commission in 1938, although for some counties one or more surveys are missing. Pender's Census was re-published by Clearfield in 1997, with supplementary material from 1660-61 Poll Tax ordinances [35].

On 30 July 1641, with the prospect of civil war looming over the English horizon, the House of Commons asked all males over the age of eighteen, among other oaths, to maintain "the true Reformed Protestant Religion", "His Majestie's Royal Person" and "the Privileges of Parliament". Conducted on a national basis these Protestation Returns, now kept in the House of Lords Record Office, are particular-ly useful in determining on which side an ancestor stood at this period in history. The returns list not only those who agreed, and thus signed or made their mark, but also those who refused to sign. For some counties every return has survived [36] and in many cases transcripts have been made and published in recent years; how-ever, for other counties all are lost.

For 1651 another estimate of the population of Guernsey (see 1615) has been made and similarly commented upon.

From the mid-seventeenth century many further taxes were imposed and the consequent lists of the taxpayers are most useful sources of names. The sums which were paid in many cases indicate the financial worth of either the individuals concerned or the property which they occupied or owned - in any case such inform-ation is invaluable in the compilation of a family history. The range of taxes includes poll tax listings from 1660 to 1700 which had their origins in similar taxes imposed from 1222. These poll tax lists contain the names of adults and children over 16 years of age, although sometimes only the numbers of children, not their names, are stated. The originals of many of these lists have found their way into county record offices, although the PRO also holds a considerable number.

The names of those who in 1661 contributed towards a "free and voluntary gift" on a county-by-county basis appear on the lists that were compiled in that year. It is believed that public collections were made on market days. The original lists have been deposited in county record offices. The "gift" was to celebrate the return of Charles II to the throne, and so the names of the donors are likely to be only those who supported the restoration of the monarchy, or those who believed it expedient to display their names on such lists. Original documents for over thirty counties, including some in Ulster (1662-66), are known to be extant.

In 1662, and annually until 1688, the ancient Saxon Fumage Tax, based on the number of chimneys at a dwelling, was revived as a Hearth Tax; but this time the tax was payable in two instalments, on Lady Day and on Michaelmas Day, on the number of firehearths or fireplaces, unless the occupier was exempt by reason of poverty. Strictly, there were two lists generated on each occasion, the assessment of the amount payable, and the return which carried the amount actually paid. The surviving documents do not readily distinguish one from the other and all are generally referred to as returns. Those for 1662 listed only the taxable hearths but after 1663 all hearths were itemised. The original lists have been deposited in the relevant county record offices and are usually catalogued among the Quarter Sessions material. However, duplicate copies were made centrally by the Exchequer clerks in London and these duplicates, which are deposited in the PRO are considerably easier to read. JSWG has provided a county-by-county directory [37] of the location of Hearth Tax assessments and returns. The Hearth Tax returns for 1664, which were compiled on Lady Day, are the most complete. Returns for some Irish counties between 1663 and 1669 indicate that the tax was collected here also.

The Hearth Tax, which was levied at two shillings per fireplace, should have raised £1,200,000 per year but there was considerable opposition and much evasion, and it even resulted in riots in Bristol and London. In the event some years realised a mere £170,000 and at the most only £700,000 a year was raised. Few officials bothered to collect the tax after 1674 and it was formally abolished in 1688. But the lists do contain names of individuals with the number of fireplaces on which they were taxed (or from which they were exempt). The numbers of hearths have been used by statisticians to calculate the populations of communities at this period, the usual multiplier being 4.5 times the number of listed hearths.

In 1665 Bills of Mortality were instituted to provide data on deaths due to the plague. These continued, in some areas on an annual basis, long after 1665 and provide colourful descriptions of causes of death in the seventeenth and, in some areas, later centuries. The data, however, was derived somewhat unskillfully, in many cases from parish registers, and no allowance appears to have been made for nonconformists who failed to register most baptisms and some burials. Thus the data is not always very accurate even though the Bills do make fascinating reading.

At Coleridge, Devon in 1670 a subscription was raised for Turkish prisoners of war. Those who contributed were listed by name, so providing an indication of those with some means in the parish, or at least those with some sympathy towards the prisoners. The original subscription list has been deposited in the Devon Record Office in Plymouth.

On 8 October 1673 the inhabitants within the manor and parish of Swindon, Wiltshire were listed. The names of the jurors and homage that served in the court that year were also specifically mentioned. The list may now be consulted in Swindon reference library.

The most widely documented census of 1676 is the Compton or Sheldon enumeration. Compton, who was a Bishop of London living from 1632 to 1713, collected some comprehensive statistics on families living in England and Wales on behalf of Gilbert Sheldon who was Archbishop of Canterbury from 1663 to 1677. Hence either name is applied to this parish-by-parish listing which is mainly numbers of conformists, Papists and Nonconformists. However, not a few returns name the Dissenters whilst other returns name all the inhabitants of particular parishes. Some original returns are in the Canterbury Cathedral Archives [38], others are in Lambeth Palace [39] and there is an eighteenth century copy of the returns for the Province of Canterbury in the William Salt Library [40] at Stafford.

The background history to the Compton Census was discussed in detail by Dr Thomas Richards in 1927, then recently appointed Librarian of University College, Bangor, in a supplement [41] to the annual publication of the Honourable Society of Cymmrodorion for that year; whilst the greater part of that article made particular reference to Welsh archdeaconries and parishes, the first fifteen or so pages explain the generic origins of this enumeration. A comprehensive volume [42] by Dr E Anne Whiteman in 1986 provided an even more comprehensive account. Some of the returns and surveys resulting from Compton's census are described below.

An analysis of the results for the Dioceses of Canterbury and Rochester was made by Christopher William Chalkin and made available by the Records Publication Committee of the Kent Archaeological Society [43] in 1960.

The listing of the names of the inhabitants of Wrotham and Stansted, Kent, is an example conducted in Shoreham Deanery in 1676. A commentary on this census was also published by the Kent Archaeological Society [44].

On 7 April 1676, Francis Nicholson, the curate-in-charge at Goodnestone-next-Wingham, Kent, commenced an account of his parishioners, according to their "families, quality and religion". Nicholson used the term "quality" to distinguish between gentlemen, yeomen, tradesmen, labourers and poor men. This most useful listing of named inhabitants was probably prompted by Bishop Compton's request. Nicholson's original account is deposited in the Canterbury Cathedral Library.

A similar listing of parishes and the number of communicants, together with the numbers of Catholics, Quakers and Dissenters, was prepared in 1676 for the Diocese of Carlisle. A commentary on this was published by Francis Godwin James [45] in 1952 with an additional comment on the apparent discrepancy between the numbers of "persons of age to communicate" and of those confirmed. The returns for Lincolnshire were transcribed by Arthur S Langley and published in *Lincolnshire Notes and Queries* [46] in 1920, those for Nottinghamshire were published [47] in 1924 by the Thoroton Society, while those for Suffolk appeared in that county's Local History Council publication, *Suffolk Review* [48] in 1966. A reference to the Peterborough Diocesan returns, where the headings appear as numbers of "Familyes, Prns young and old, Popish Recusants and Obstinate separatists" was published in *Local Population Studies* [49] in 1973, although the figures for only six parishes were transcribed.

At Clayworth, Nottinghamshire, the rector, William Sampson, conducted his own census of his parish in 1676 and again in 1688, providing what appear to be comprehensive lists of the inhabitants. The 1676 census was more than likely prompted by Compton's request as Sampson took his survey on 9 April; but it appears to have begun life as a subscription list on behalf of the inhabitants of Northampton who were suffering from the devastating effects of a fire which had swept through that town. Both the 1676 and the 1688 censuses of Clayworth, but especially the former, have been the subjects of extensive studies by population scholars [50] who have compared them with other local lists and drawn numerous conclusions. Abstracts from the 1676 list are, therefore, quoted in many articles, while a complete copy of the original may be found in the county archives [51].

1677 saw the publication by Samuel Lee of *A Collection of the Names of the Merchants Living In and About the City of London.* Although by no means a real census this publication was the first English directory and does provide names, occupations and addresses. Over successive years trade and private directories were published for counties, cities, towns and villages throughout the British Isles.

In Ireland *The Gentleman's and Citizen's Almanack* began publication in Dublin in 1736. Whilst such directories are beyond the scope of this Cameo, their "census like" content should not be overlooked. Descriptive accounts including the publications of Sketchley, White, Bains, Hunt, Pigot, Slater and Kelly with their historical background to 1856 were related in 1932 by Charles WF Goss [52] for the London area, and in 1950 and 1984 by Jane E Norton [53] for the remainder of England and Wales, and in 1897 by Edward Evans for Irish directories [54].

Lists of Papists were again made in 1680, these lists now being kept at the House of Lords Record Office [55]. *The Eleventh Report of the Historical Manuscripts Commission* in describing this holding indicates the number of Papists in each county (Northamptonshire had 8 whilst Monmouthshire had 189), but for some counties (eg Herefordshire) the names of individuals are given in the abstract.

In 1684 lists were made by ministers in seventeen parishes in Wigtownshire and Minnigaff in Scotland of all the inhabitants over the age of 12. The purpose was probably to gather information on the potential military strength in the area relating to the Covenanters, the more extreme of whom were strongly opposed to the restored monarch, Charles II, in his attitude towards the Solemn League and Covenant. For some of the seventeen parishes, relationships between individuals were noted. A transcription of these lists was edited by William Scott and published by the Scottish Record Society [56] in 1916.

Also in 1684 a census including the names and ages of individuals was held at Chilvers Coton in Warwickshire. The original returns are in the record office in Warwick. Additionally in 1684 a valuation was conducted in the parishes of Box, Ditchridge and Haslebury, Wiltshire. Names of adult males were included in the lists made at the time, thus providing a pseudo-census for those parishes. The original valuation is deposited in the Wiltshire Record Office in Trowbridge.

The Roman Catholic Archbishop Leyburn of Westminster travelled from London to beyond Newcastle upon Tyne in 1687, visiting many places in Lancashire and returning through the Midlands. He confirmed 20,000 persons in the Catholic faith and recorded their names (and in a few cases dates of the services) in his Confirmation Register. This was published in 1997 by the North West Catholic History Society.

Abstracts from surveys of London, taken for various purposes in 1687 and 1690 were quoted by Dr Richard Price [57] in his *Observations on Reversionary Payments* in its various editions from 1771 to 1812. The number of houses, but not families, in London in 1687 calculated from Hearth Tax Returns (*qv*) was first referred to by Sir William Petty in *Political Arithmetic* (pp 74 and 79); in Dr Davenant's *Works* (Vol 1 p 38) the 1690 figures for London (and all other counties) were analysed. Price became deeply involved in writing and presenting papers, particularly to the Royal Society, on various aspects of population figures. He not only drew on surveys, such as those for London of the seventeenth century, but he encouraged many colleagues in the eighteenth century to personally undertake other surveys and supply him with their results. Many such surveys, enumerations and censuses used by Price in his theses are referred to below.

A Parliamentary Act of 1694 for the registration of births, marriages and burials became effective from 1 May 1695 for a period of five years. The purpose was to tax each registration in order to raise revenue "for carrying on the war against France with Vigour" in which England was indulging at that time. The tax was complicated in that it was graduated according to status, and the Act was complicated in that it required births to be registered within five days and the events to be recorded on certificates for each Parish, Division, Constablewick, Allotment and Place; but the Act did not state what should be written on the certificates, although it did state that they should be forwarded to the Commissioners of the Act for the first year (as for the Land Tax) and to the county justices for the remaining four years. Unfortunately the Act also failed to state what should happen to the certificates thereafter, which may explain the random survival of the returns of what is often called the *Marriage Duty Act*. The Act was further convoluted in attempting to extract duties from bachelors of 25 or over and childless widowers (but not spinsters or widows), and requiring detailed statistics on nobility and gentry. For a full description of this Act and its scale of charges see the Chapmans Records Cameo *Marriage Laws, Rites, Records and Customs* [58].

In spite of all the confusion many assessors did produce annual returns, and included the name, estate, degree, and title of each individual and how much tax was payable. Servants, women and children were also included; thus these returns, where they have survived, form excellent censuses. Unfortunately no centrally-maintained lists appear to have been kept, presumably because of the confusion as to what to do with the certificates once collected, and there are no complete lists for every county. In fact for many counties most lists have been lost, but where they do survive they offer very useful data, actually over a longer period than originally intended as the Act was not repealed until 1705, rather than the planned date of 1700.

For Lyme Regis, Dorset, lists were made in 1695, 1697, 1699, 1701, 1702 and 1703 which are now in the county record office. The 1695 listing for London and the 1696 listing for Bristol are among the most useful; both listings [59] are held locally and have been indexed and published by the respective local record societies, the former in 1966, under surnames, places and trades, the latter in 1968 under surnames. The 1698 listing for Fenny Compton, Warwickshire taken on 7 April, disappeared into private hands until 1883 when a descendant of one of the 1698 churchwardens presented the original to the rector, who kept it with the parish records; a commentary on the list (but not a transcription) was made by Philip Styles [60] in 1951, drawing comparisons with other lists. There is a similar listing for the thirty-six townships in the Wingham Petty Division of Kent, although the latter was taken during the last year that the Act was in force - 1705. The original returns for the Wingham Division have been deposited in the Kent County Archives.

A list of the inhabitants of Melbourne, Derbyshire with their "title and qualificat- ions" (actually their trades and occupations) was made in 1695, as a consequence of the *Marriage Duty Act* described above. The list states the required information, i.e. the amounts of duty paid for burials, marriages, births, bachelors and widowers, and also indicates a few individuals aged 25. During the nineteenth century the Melbourne list was discussed in an article [61] published in the *Journal of the Derbyshire Archaeological and Natural History Society*. At that time the list was held privately by Viscount Hardinge, it having been passed down in his family from an ancestor who, as a local Justice of the Peace, had signed and allowed the original assessment in 1695. Unfortunately its present whereabouts are unknown, thus illustrating the value of transcripts and copies of original documents, and the benefit of them being deposited in secure archives. A similar list for Donhead, Wiltshire has been discovered among its parish chest material, whilst one for New Romney, Kent was found in the town records.

Also in 1695 all public office holders were required by an Act of Parliament to take an oath of loyalty or Association to William and Mary and an oath that should these monarchs be assassinated by Jacobite supporters they would take revenge on them. Thus Association Oath Rolls, which contain the signatures of the loyal officers, were compiled on a county basis, in some cases subdivided into hundreds and boroughs. But these rolls were made available for any citizens of England and Wales and English colonies overseas to sign; therefore, the lists, which are now at the PRO, contain many adult males and in some cases female householders as well, such that for some areas almost complete censuses of the adult population were created. The clergy signed separate rolls which were collected and collated by deanery and diocese and these are filed this way today. The rolls for some counties have been published, those for Lancashire, for example, by Wallace Gandy in 1921, republished by the Society of Genealogists in 1985 [62]. A catalogue of extant Association Oath Rolls was prepared by Clifford Webb in 1983, later incorporated by JSWG into his Guide on the Hearth Tax [63].

Gregory King, known to many as the "Father of Population Studies", began his study on the *Natural and Political Observations upon the State and Condition of England* in 1695. Although he had completed this by the following year his observations were not published until 1802 when they appeared as an appendix to George Chambers' *An Estimate of the Comparative Strength of Great Britain*. King was not only Lancaster Herald but also a draughtsman, heraldic painter, engraver, cartographer, surveyor and architect. As a herald he would have conducted heraldic visitations and it is believed that he used the same material to calculate the population - although it is not known how. It is also possible that he took the number of houses quoted in the Hearth Tax returns (*qv*) and used a suitable multiplier to arrive at a population figure. It is more probable that he used data from the 1694 *Marriage Duty Act* returns, together with his own surveys, to derive the numbers for the population. A variety of commentaries on King's work have been published over the years [64].

In Scotland, a poll tax was imposed during 1695 by the Scottish Parliament to augment existing revenue sources; this was in order to increase the efficiency of the army and navy to combat danger from foreign and internal (including English) enemies. An earlier poll tax imposed in 1693 had been a failure. The returns for Aberdeenshire and Renfrewshire and a few scattered parishes in Scotland are in the National Archives of Scotland (NAS); those for the former county were published in two volumes in 1844 as a *List of Pollable Persons within the Shire of Aberdeen*. The information to be found in the returns is useful as they state the name, status, place of residence and occupation of every person who was over 16 and not a pauper (a burden on the parish). A commentary [65] on the returns was published in 1950.

In Dublin an exact survey of the number of inhabitants was undertaken in 1695, together with surveys for the counties of Armagh, Louth and Meath; the results of these were communicated by Captain South to the Royal Society, published in their *Philosophical Transactions* and also quoted by Price [66], as was a similar survey of Maidstone, Kent.

In 1696 a Window Tax was introduced and remained in force (with some modifications made during the reign of George III) until replaced in 1851 by a House Duty Tax, itself abolished in 1924. The Window Tax, granted to William III, was introduced initially to generate sufficient income to enable the Royal Mint to make up the deficiency caused by individuals feloniously clipping fragments off silver coins to collect and sell the silver. The tax paid for the reminting of the damaged coins and also retrieved for the treasury the value of the lost silver. Records of this tax, for which there was a separate return for each township, contain the name and address of each taxpayer, the number of windows on which tax was paid and the money collected. Hospitals, charity schools, almshouses and workhouses were also assessed as if the tax was to be applied but were each granted an exemption certificate, as were churches and chapels. Dairies and cheese-rooms were also exempt from tax so long as their windows were unglazed and their outer doors and the outside of their windows were clearly identified with large painted letters stating "Dairy" or "Cheese Room". Large windows were assessed as two. The Royal Family was also exempt from paying. Similarly to the Hearth Tax, the Window Tax offers an indication of the social status of an ancestor, as well as his abode, even though the tax was in general badly administered and many of the returns have been lost by today. Window Tax returns, whilst not prolific for most areas of the country, may be located in county record offices, in many cases filed with the Quarter Sessions records. JSWG's *Land and Window Tax Assessments* [67] offers a county-by-county guide to the extant returns.

In the Bedfordshire village of Pavenham a census was taken in 1699 within Stevington manor; the names of the villagers and in some cases their occupations were recorded in the parish register. This is now in the county record office in Bedford, as is a similar listing of 1712 for Houghton Conquest. Although both of these were known locally as collections of King's Certainty Money, they were probably Poll Tax listings, the name being confused with the colloquial term - Certain Money - for the manorial Common Fine. Ship Money collection lists in Bedfordshire are also similarly confused with land or poll tax lists. Debate on this confusion, with an exhaustive account of other listings for Bedfordshire, is given by Colin Chapman as the opening chapter in *Essays in Honour of Patricia Bell*, published by the Bedfordshire Historical Record Society in 1993 as Volume 72 in its annual series.

As the seventeenth century progressed, parish incumbents and catechists of the Church of Scotland made notes of who had been questioned or examined on their understanding of the catechism. Some recorded the names of all parishioners in an Examination or Catechism Roll, thus providing a census-type listing. Several rolls have survived, now in the National Archives of Scotland or in Scottish Regional Archives. One parish in Perthshire, St Madoes, has a surviving Catechism Roll from even the sixteenth century.

4. Eighteenth century listings: 1700 to 1750

Enumerations of the inhabitants of Liverpool appear to have been taken every decade from 1700 until 1770 at least, as the figures were quoted in 1773 by Dr W Enfield in the second edition of *An Essay towards the history of Leverpool*. Enfield was a 'lecturer on the Belles Lettres in the Academy at Warrington' and may have influenced the undertaking of a survey there as well when his book was published (see 1773 below when yet another enumeration for Liverpool was undertaken). Dr J Aikin also commented on the population of Liverpool during the eighteenth century in his book on Manchester (page 335 *et seq*) published in 1795 (see 1781 below).

In Ireland, the Freemen of Cork City were listed from 1700 to 1752. This list is now preserved in the INA [69].

A census was undertaken of communicants within the ancient parish of Stoke-upon-Trent in 1701. Four years later Samuel Paulson, the parish clerk, copied the details which are now in the Staffordshire Record Office [70]. The copy, which unfortunately appears to be of only part of the total parish, lists the names and ages of the communicants by household; the head is named first followed by his wife, the children and the servants. Widows, single women, and adult brothers and sisters who acted as joint heads of households are also identified.

Estate Lists, similar to the manorial surveys of the seventeenth century, provide names of tenants. A typical listing is that for 1703-4 of the tenants of Robert Craiges for the parishes of Kildallon and Killeshandra, County Cavan, Ireland. The tenants' names were abstracted by Brian de Breffny and published in *The Irish Ancestor* in 1976 [71].

From 1703 (until 1838) lists were compiled in Ireland of those who joined the Church of Ireland as converts from Roman Catholicism to the Anglican faith. The period from 1760 to 1790 shows the greatest numbers of names on these Convert Rolls. The lists, edited by Eileen O'Byrne, were published by the Irish Manuscripts Commission in 1981 and are available in the National Library of Ireland (NLI).

A population survey of Minehead, Somerset, which was undertaken in 1705, is referred to by John Collinson, the vicar of Long Ashton, [72] in his *History and Antiquities of the County of Somerset...*, published in 1791. The number of houses and their location were included in this survey although the whereabouts of the original are not now known.

In 1705 Deputy Lieutenants were required, by an Order in Council of 18 January 1705, to supply statistics on Papists. For some counties names were compiled into lists which are now among the House of Lords records; however, for most counties no Papists were located and a typical response [73], such as that from Anglesey, stated "we are so happy in this county that we have never a Papist but one, and he is a person of mean fortune and an old man ....". Shortly afterwards, on 2 March 1705, apparently as a result of the poor response to the first request, the House of Lords asked archbishops and bishops to supply the same statistics; on this occasion the responses were more fruitful, although not all bishops appear to have reacted positively. Those who did often provided names of the Papists, and for the Diocese of London occupations were also given; the latter lists are today in the Guildhall Library [74]. Others, such as those for the Diocese of Chester which state names and occupations, have been published from originals held in the House of Lords Record Office [75].

The regular Visitations of the Archbishops throughout the eighteenth century in many instances contain numbers of Papists in each parish. In a few of these Visitations, names of the Papists appear. A number of the returns compiled by the ecclesiastical clerks have been transcribed by bodies such as the Catholic Record Society; more locally interested groups, the Yorkshire Archaeological Society for example, have published the returns for their particular area [76].

The potential growth in Roman Catholicism was of such concern to some clerics that on 4 August 1706 the Archbishop of Canterbury was persuaded to secure an Order in Council requiring every incumbent to take an exact account of the number of Papists and reputed Papists in his parish; the incumbent was further required to state the Papists' qualities, estates and places of abode. This Order also enquired what advowsons or rights of presentation or donation of churches, benefices or schools were in the disposition of Papists or reputed Papists. The House of Lords Record Office holds the diocesan summaries for many dioceses, although there are some locally held lists in county record offices [77]. The majority of these lists and summaries have been transcribed and many have been published by the Catholic Record Society [78].

Between 1706 and 1721 surveys for the Diocese of Lincoln were produced by the incumbents or archdeacons between 1706 and 1721, obviously in response to the 1706 Order in Council. That taken by the Church authorities at Boston, Lincolnshire in 1709 may well be an example of the Papist survey request. However, in the case of Boston, neither the original returns nor any analysis appear to have survived although the survey itself and the total figure of the population are mentioned in Thompson's *History of Boston*, published in 1856.

A list of householders in Downpatrick, County Down, Ireland was made in 1708; this appears in R Edward Parkinson's *City of Down from its earliest days*, published in Belfast in 1928.

From 1711 until 1835 lists for an annual tax or assessment (known colloquially as a cess) were compiled for St Michan's parish, Dublin, Ireland. These lists were entered in the Annual Cess Applotment Books, now in the library of the Representative Church Body (RCB) in Dublin.

The 1712 listing for Houghton Conquest, Bedfordshire has already been mentioned (see 1699).

The numbers of families in each of the Lancashire parishes of Oldham, Chaderton (*sic*), Royton and Crompton in 1714, and comparisons with the numbers in 1789 and 1792 were made by Dr J Aikin in 1795 in his book (p 242) on Manchester (see 1781 below).

A Parliamentary Act of 1715 (1 Geo III c.55) required all Papists in England and Wales to register their land ownership (real estate) with county justices, who sent certified copies of the Roman Catholics' names with alleged values of their land to commissioners in London. Abstracts from the register, now in the PRO, with a copy in the BL, were published in 1745, 1746, 1862 and 1885. The 1885 work, edited by Edgar E Estcourt and John Orelbar Payne, intriguingly entitled *English Catholic Nonjurors of 1715*, is the most comprehensive and includes some added genealogical and biographical notes. A list of Protestant males between the ages of 16 and 60 living in the parish of St John, Kilkenny City, Ireland was drawn up in 1715; this list is now in the INA. A not dissimilar 1731 listing of all Protestants in Shrule, County Longford, Ireland is in the library of the RCB.

Register Rolls of Papists were kept by the Ely diocesan authorities from 1716 to 1744, and as such have remained among the bishops' records; in most cases where they survive, these are now in the pertinent county archives. A similar series from 1723-48 for the Diocese of London is in the Guildhall Library [79]. Numbers of people on the Hertfordshire lists were most competently discussed in 1964 [80] by Lionel Munby, together with many other figures available in a variety of ecclesiastical sources, in one of the publications of that county's Local History Council.

In 1723 many individuals swore an Oath of Allegiance before their county justices "pursuant to the late act 9 Georgii Regis", thus providing not only a list of names of potential ancestors and their "places of aboad", but also their declared loyalty to the Crown. For most counties the lists have been filed with the Quarter Sessions material in the county archives; for Cheshire, four small volumes of these lists survive among the sessions records, whereas at York there is a list of 1,800 inhabitants, with occupations, in the City Council Minute Book.

An "Account of the number of families, communicants and souls in Wakefield [Yorkshire] town and parish, taken December 9th 1723", was drawn up to justify the demand for a second church in the town - finally achieved in 1795. The list identifies the names of heads of households, the total number in each family, and the number of communicants, and includes some biographical footnotes. It was prepared as a sixteen-page Appendix to Thomas Taylor's *History of the Rectory Manor of Wakefield* but not published until 1978 [81].

At Puddleton, Dorset a census was taken of the parishioners in 1724-25 by the vicar. The originals of this return are now deposited in the county record office at Dorchester.

In 1727, Guernsey was again (see 1615 and 1651) the subject of an estimate of the population figures. This, like those of the earlier estimates, was quoted by Dury in his article referred to above. An election list for County Galway, Ireland for this year was published by the Galway Historical and Archaeological Society in 1976.

An enumeration was undertaken in each parish at Cambridge in 1728, probably by Bowtell in preparation for his *History of Cambridge*. The work, which was intended to comprise several volumes, was never published but his draft notes were deposited with his other manuscripts in the library of Downing College, Cambridge. The total population figure of 6,422 in Bowtell's work was quoted [82] by Charles Henry Cooper, who also rearranged the parish lists into alphabetical order, in his *Annals of Cambridge*, published in 1852.

In 1730, for Douglas, Isle of Man, a list was drawn up of the names of residents ("housekeepers" is the term used in the original document although in many cases an apparent husband and wife are both named as the housekeeper); the numbers of their children, servants, and lodgers and strangers were also given. This list, edited with some introductory notes by William Harrison, was printed in 1878 but published [83] in 1880 as the second volume of *Manx Miscellanies* by the Manx Society. The published list has some 35 fewer households than the original, now in the Douglas archives. Within the introductory notes is reference to an account of the number of souls in Douglas from a paper of Bishop Wilson in 1726 and also to a similar return by the Clergy in 1757; the latter itemises numbers of married couples, widowers, widows, adult single men, adult single women, males under 16 and females under 16. There is also reference to the same breakdown of population made on 29 January 1784 by Thomas W J Woods, Vicar of Braddan, by order of Edward Smith, the Governor. The *Commissioners Report* for 1792, Appendix B Nos 89, 90, & 91 quoted the figures.

The registers of Papists requested by the House of Lords for the diocesan authorities have already been referred to. In some cases, though, they are mixed with the returns made in preparation for the ecclesiastical visitations. Those of 1735 sent to Archbishop Blackburn for the diocese of York are a good example; transcripts were published by the Catholic Record Society in 1907 [84], and the returns for York city and part of Ainsty were published with comment, in Vol III (pages 4-8, 84-8 and 177-80) and Vol IV (pages 34-6) of the *Northern Genealogist* in 1900-01.

In 1736, by order of the Town Burgesses, an enumeration was made at Sheffield to ascertain the population of the city prior to a petition being presented in Parliament to make St Paul's Church parochial. The number of families and individuals in the township of Sheffield, in Brightside, Byerlow, Attercliffe-cum-Darnall, Ecclesall and the two Hallams was recorded. In his *Hallamshire*, Joseph Hunter [85] has quoted figures from a manuscript of Dr Thomas Short regarding this enumeration.

On Jersey, on 10 June 1737, an enumeration was conducted of the numbers of houses and inhabitants in each parish. The numbers of men, women and children under 14 and those at sea *"en service"* and *"a Terreneuve"* were identified separately. The original document, which is in the University Library, Cambridge [86], has only ten of the twelve parishes, even though its title clearly states *"chaque paroisse"* (each parish). For seven of the ten parishes the statistics are subdivided into *vingtaines*. No names are included in the parish enumerations which total 13,642 persons. There is a copy of the original in the Library of the Channel Islands Family History Society.

In 1737 Dr William Maitland [87] made an estimate "with incredible pains" "from the parish books" of the number of houses in London. Similar estimates and attempts to distinguish cottages from houses were made in subsequent years (1758, 1761, 1765, 1777, for example) from the returns of the window tax surveyors. Papers on these figures were read at meetings of the Royal Society and published in their *Philosophical Transactions* in 1756, 1758 and 1760. Price further referred to this data in his *Observations*; although Maitland had originally published his figures (together with others for 1627 to 1635 and for 1728 to 1737) in 1739 in his own *History of London from its foundation by the Romans to the present time....with the several accounts of Westminster, Middlesex, Southwark and other parts within the Bill of Mortality.*

A list of the names of Tithe-payers of 1737 in Drumcree, County Armagh, Ireland is held in the NLI, as is a list of the Freeholders in all of County Armagh.

An account of the number of inhabitants of Chelmsford, Essex in 1738 was mentioned by Philip Morant in his *History and Antiquities of the County of Essex...*, published in 1768 [88]. Morant quotes only the total population and the original survey does not appear to be extant.

An enumeration of 1739 for Nottingham was described by George Charles Deering in his *Nottinghamia vetus et nova, or an historical account of the ancient and present state of....Nottingham....* in 1751. Whilst Deering refers to the numbers of houses and their location, as well as the total population figures, the original returns do not appear to have survived. An index to Deering's work by Rupert Cecil Chicken was published in 1899.

In 1740 the names of Protestant householders in the Irish counties of Antrim, Armagh, Donegal, Down, Londonderry and Tyrone were listed by parish and barony. Regrettably, none of the surviving lists is complete and only householders' names are given. The original lists are now distributed between the NLI, the RCB, the Genealogical Office in Dublin and the PRONI.

At Aynho in Northamptonshire a list of names of the families and numbers of persons was made on 30 December 1740. Against each family on the list the number of servants and the number of family members were identified and the total number of 125 families, 82 servants and 567 persons given at the end of the list. A check was evidently made subsequently as in another hand a further four families were identified and added to the list. On two sheets of otherwise plain paper this list is amongst the parochial documents of Aynho in the Northamptonsire Archives.

In 1741 the inhabitants of Farnham, Surrey were enumerated. At that time Farnham was a mere village with less than 2,000 people - a sharp contrast to the Farnham of today. This enumeration was referred to nearly forty years later by William Wales in his *An Inquiry into the Present State of the Population of England and Wales* published in 1781 (*qv*). The original document from which Wales quoted appears to be missing.

At Olveston, Gloucestershire 'the number and names of the inhabitants... which do actually live upon the spot [were] taken in the year 1742 by Chris: Shute Vicar'. In fact Rev Cristopher (*sic*) Shute listed only the names of the 125 heads of the households and indicated "his wife" and the numbers of servants and children in the tythings of Olveston and Tockington. An article on this census, now in Bristol Record Office, appeared, with the inhabitants' names, in the fifteenth quarterly *Journal of the Bristol and Avon Family History Society* in the Spring of 1979.

A survey of the numbers of families and inhabitants, including the numbers of males and females, was conducted in 1743 for Edinburgh's parish of St Cuthbert. This was referred to in 1753 by William Maitland [89] in his *History of Edinburgh from its Foundation to the Present Time....* and was further quoted by Price [90].

Population figures for Gloucester in 1743 appear among the Furneys papers [91] in the Bodleian Library, Oxford. The figures, which included the number of married couples and the number of houses, were published in 1819 by Thomas Dudley Fosbroke in his *Original History of the City of Gloucester.... including also the original papers of.... R Bigland* [92]. The Visitation Returns required by the diocesan authorities are useful for York diocese for 1743; the information sent to Archbishop Herring included details on Papists and has been published by the Yorkshire Archaeological Society [93] in four of its volumes.

A list of the inhabitants of Stanton St Bernard, Wiltshire was made in 1744. This list is to be found in the Wiltshire Record Office at Trowbridge.

A list of voters in County Clare, Ireland was compiled in 1745; the original is held by Trinity College, Dublin. A Poll Book for the same year, showing for whom the voters exercised their franchise, for County Wicklow, Ireland is in the PRONI.

In 1746 an enumeration was conducted in Northampton which included the numbers of houses and inhabitants. For the parishes of All Saints and St Giles the surveys detailed males and females, servants, lodgers and children; for St Peter's parish the numbers were broken down only to males and females and for St Sepulchre's to adults and children. Price subsequently [94] thanked Mr Lawton for obtaining the figures. The results of this survey were the subject of some detailed discussion over a century later in 1847 by William Farr [95] who was then the Registrar General; in his *Report for Commissioners*, Farr commented on Northampton Life Tables and the results of Bills of Mortality both generally and specifically.

Detail on the population of Hertford was collected in 1747 as it was felt that the existing estimated figures were out of date. A letter to the *Gentleman's Magazine* [96] in July of that year advised that the correspondent had undertaken this survey "by particular enquiry" in the ancient town in the parishes of St Andrew, All Saints and St John. The survey distinguished between members of the Established Church, Dissenters and Quakers.

A carriage tax was re-introduced in 1747 and remained in force until 1782. Carriages with four wheels were taxed at a higher rate than those with two, and two wheeled carriages drawn by two horses incurred a higher duty than those drawn by one horse. Carts were also taxed unless such carts were used in the affairs of husbandry or carriage of goods in the course of trade, in which case the words "Common Stage Cart" and the name and address of the owner had to be painted on the side of the cart. Whilst not a census, the lists of those who paid this tax do furnish names of individuals and imply their social standing; the vast majority of the population could not afford to own or operate a carriage or cart on which this duty was payable, thus those whose names do appear on the carriage tax lists would have been in the upper stratum of society.

In 1748 a survey was undertaken of the numbers of houses and families in the city and liberties of Edinburgh. Similarly to the 1743 survey (*qv*) this was referred to by Maitland [97] and Price [98].

Thomas Jefferys engraved a number of maps between 1748 and 1750, particularly for towns in the Midlands of England. Whilst he utilised information furnished by various surveyors, in many cases Jefferys included population figures for the towns which he depicted on his maps. For example, the numbers of houses and inhabitants in Coventry (1748) and in Birmingham (1750) were quoted on the maps which he engraved from Bradford's surveys of these two towns. He similarly quoted the numbers of houses and inhabitants on the maps he engraved from Isaac Taylor's surveys in 1750 for Wolverhampton, Staffordshire, in 1751 for Oxford and in 1757 for Hereford.

An ecclesiastical census was taken in the Church of Ireland diocese of Elphin in 1749. This included parts of the counties of Galway, Roscommon (best coverage) and Sligo. Names of householders, their religion and the numbers, sex and religion of their children and servants are noted. The surviving returns are in the INA.

In 1749 Cambridge was subject to another (see 1728) enumeration, but for this year the numbers of houses, besides the breakdown of the population figures into parishes within the city, were identified. The figures were "collected from house to house" and published in Edmund Carter's *History of the County of Cambridge from the Earliest Account to the Present Time* in 1753 [99]. It would appear that at least one of the original collections "from house to house" has survived; this contains names of householders and numbers in each house for St Benedict's parish, and is in the county record office at Cambridge [100]. Two other listings containing names, for the parishes of St Giles and St Peter, which include "the number of souls in every family, and the religion they profess" are stuck in the back covers of a copy of *The history and antiquities of Barnwell Abbey and of Sturbridge Fair* which has been deposited in the Bodleian Library, Oxford [101]. However, comparing the numbers on these lists with Carter's figures it would appear that these two listings were made around 1760.

On 30 April 1750 a list was compiled of 184 French Protestants "that have left France for their religion and are now residing in the Island of Jersey". The purpose of compiling such a list appears to have been to identify to the English government suitable "foreign Protestants" to send to Nova Scotia as acceptable settlers in that colony. The English who had been sent to Halifax the previous year had not stayed in the town, and the authorities were anxious for the colony to succeed, but not as a Roman Catholic settlement. It would appear, however, that the people listed were not sent to Nova Scotia, and thus put down roots in Jersey. The original of this list, which is in the Colonial Office records [102] for Nova Scotia, contains the names, occupations and ages in years and months of the French Protestants. A transcript was made by Terrence M Punch and published in the *Channel Islands Family History Journal* [103] in 1988, although there are copies in the Channel Islands Family History Society library and that of La Société Jersiaise, St Helier, Jersey.

A survey was undertaken in 1750 for Shrewsbury, Shropshire by John Leigh who also, similarly to the work undertaken for Northampton in 1746, prepared Bills of Mortality. Leigh, however, included an analysis of the age of the inhabitants of the town as well as the number of houses and their parochial location. The enumeration resulting from the 1750 survey was included in the 1754 Bill for Shrewsbury. For the parish of Holy Cross the numbers of families and inhabitants were further recorded by the vicar, Rev William Gorsuch; he also kept detailed notes of the numbers of males under 10, females under 10, males between 70 and 80, females between 70 and 80, males over 80 and females over 80. Gorsuch repeated his surveys every five years until 1780, making his results available to Price and the Royal Society [104], which published his findings in 1761, 1771 and 1782.

5. Eighteenth century listings: 1751 to 1774

John Browning of Barton Hill, Bristol calculated the number of inhabitants of the City of Bristol in 1751 "from the burials over a period of ten years, and from the number of houses from the 1751 land-tax". He obviously took a great deal of care with his calculations because he "consulted the praecentor of the college, the ministers of the several 17 parish churches, the register keepers of the several quakers' cemeteries, the several Anabaptists' cemeteries, the Jews' newly erected cemetery" for the ten years from 1741 to 1750. Using a figure of six people to a house he concluded that the Bristol population was 43,692 from the number of houses compared with 43,275 from the number of burials. Browning's results were communicated in 1753 by Henry Baker to the Royal Society which published [105] them in 1754. Population data were not Browning's only interest and he had earlier (12 September 1751) forwarded details to the Royal Society on Lewis Hopkin, a 15 year-old Welsh boy exhibited in Bristol who weighed thirteen pounds and was two feet seven inches tall.

In July 1752 a civil survey was undertaken in the city of Norwich. The numbers of married couples and the number of houses were included in the original returns which are in the Norfolk Record Office. Price quoted [106] the numbers of families and inhabitants in his *Observations*.

Copies of a 1753 Poll Book for County Armagh, Ireland are in several Irish libraries. At Liverpool a survey of the number of houses was made, also in 1753; reference was made to this by Price alongside the Norwich enumeration of the previous year.

1753 should have been one of the major milestones in the history of British censuses. It was in this year that Thomas Potter, a son of the late Archbishop of Canterbury, introduced his *Population Bill*, putting some far-reaching proposals before Parliament. The tabled Bill was descriptively entitled *A Bill, with the Amendments, for Taking and Registering an annual Account of the total Number of People, and the total Number of Marriages, Births and Deaths; and also the total Number of Poor receiving Alms from every Parish, and extraparochial Place, in Great Britain*. The opening paragraphs further explained: "Whereas it will be of publick Utility, that the total Number of People within this Realm, together with the progressive Increase or Diminution thereof, as either may respectively happen; and also the total Number of Poor receiving Alms from every Parish, or extraparochial Place; be annually taken and registered: And whereas great Inconveniencies have arisen from the present defective manner in which parochial Registers are formed, and the loose and uncertain Method in which they are kept and preserved; whereby the Evidence of Descents is frequently lost and rendered precarious: Be it therefore

enacted ...... the Overseers of the Poor, for the Time being, of every Parish, ...
shall proceed from House to House to every House within their respective Parish or
District; and shall demand and take an Account of the Number of People who at
that time shall be, and, for the Space of Twelve Hours next preceding, shall have
been, personally resident and actually dwelling therein ......".

Potter met with much opposition, not only within Parliament, and a number of
pamphlets were published criticising his Bill. One, in particular, which was
produced later in 1753 is worthy of note; running to several sheets, on the fifteenth
page is stated : "You mention, that the ascertaining the Genealogy and Descents,
may be of great Use; Our Ancestors did not think so; when they bought off the
Courts of Ward, and, inquisitio post mortem, they looked upon this registering of
every Man's Death and Birth by the Officers of the Crown, to be a high Badge of
Slavery, and so destructive to the Liberties of a free People, that they gave Excise
to get rid of this Egyptian Bondage; but you say they are only now obliged to
register with the Parson of the Parish: And why so? Are we to give to the Priests
what our Ancestors refused to the King? Why should the Dissenter register with the
Parson of the Parish, and not with the Minister of his own Congregation? Why
should not the Jew be allowed to register with his own Priest? Why should not the
Nobility be allowed to register in the Herald's-Office? And as for Descent of the
Poor, what need they to register? What signifies Genealogy to poor Labourers and
Manufacturers, and they are twenty to one of those to whom Genealogy may be of
Use, yet are all to pay to the Priest of the Parish? As for Successions, and the Times
when Youth comes of Age, we find that they do take Possession of their Estates,
and we find few Inconveniencies; and if some Disputes have arisen, a few Inconveniencies can be no Objection to a general Law, since no general Law can be
without few Inconveniencies."

Correspondence in the *Gentleman's Magazine* during November and December
1753, led particularly by William Thornton, argued strongly against Potter's
proposals (the support was permitted very little column space). But two arguments
finally disposed of Potter's Bill: it was felt that a census and its published results
would reveal England's weakness in terms of its population structure to her
potential enemies, but more drastically the opponents recounted the fate of the
Children of Israel as described in the *First Book of Chronicles* [107] in the *Old
Testament*: when David had attempted to number the tribes - conduct a census - the
wrath of God had been brought upon them. Having no wish to cause a similar fate
to eighteenth century Great Britain, the 1753 *Population Bill* wavered and then
when parliamentary time ran out it was abandoned.

But the seeds of interest had been sown, and after 1753 public debate on population
figures for England and Wales intensified, so catalysing the enthusiasm for individuals to conduct either simple enumerations or even complex censuses in their locality. In 1754, for example, a population survey was undertaken in the parish of
Stockport, Cheshire by the ecclesiastical authorities. Religious affiliation and

location in the parish were given on the original survey which is in the Bodleian Library. There is, however, a copy in Stockport Public Library and commentaries [108] have been published on this particular survey.

An *Account of the Number of People in Scotland in the Year 1755* was prepared by Dr Alexander Webster, minister of Tolbooth Church, Edinburgh; however, it was not published until 1952 when James Gray Kyd's commentary on Webster's work appeared in one of the annual volumes of the Scottish History Society [109]. Kyd included a transcript of the census of the 892 parishes in Scotland. The census actually comprised a numerical analysis of ministers, Papists, Protestants and fighting men in each parish, for which the length and breadth were also stated. Whilst 1755 appears in Webster's title to his document, the original manuscripts of which are now in the National Library of Scotland, it is more likely that most of the population figures refer to 1750. Webster was in correspondence with Price in 1771 regarding this enumeration as demonstrated in Price's [110] *Observations* (where he quoted estimated numbers of Papists and Protestants made "with labour and expence" by Rev Dr Webster) and confirmed by A J Youngson, who published a short article [111] on Webster and his census in 1962.

There are some fascinating listings of "Poor and Pious Parishioners" of Bradeley, Staffordshire in its parish registers. The names are given of those to whom Bibles and prayer books were given in 1755, 1763 and 1772.

Rev William Brackenridge in London began some heated correspondence by publishing an article in the *Philosophical Transactions of the Royal Society* [112] in 1755. He claimed that London's population had fallen since earlier that century, a claim later extended to the whole country. This was refuted by Rev Richard Forster of Great Shefford in Berkshire also in *Philosophical Transactions*; after a while the editors curtailed the claims and counter claims but the opponents continued their correspondence privately between themselves, occasionally involving third parties. Some of this correspondence has been deposited in the British Library [113].

A survey taken at Stroud, Gloucestershire in 1756, which was quoted in 1779 by Samuel Rudder in his *New History of Gloucestershire...* and that at Southampton taken in 1757, referred to in the *Southampton Herald* for 18 June 1825, may also have been initiated by the Royal Society's publication. In Belfast on 1 January 1757 a survey was undertaken of the number of looms, houses and inhabitants. This survey was referred to by Price [114] who revealed that of the population 7,993 were Protestant and 556 were Papists. On 21 March 1757 Isaac Taylor published, as an inset to a map of the city, population figures for Hereford, listed by streets, also noting the numbers of houses. It was Taylor who had published a map of Oxford in 1751 bearing the population of that city, before public debate became inflamed.

The 1757 enumeration of Ackworth, Yorkshire was probably associated with the debate; it was certainly quoted by William Wales [115] (see below, 1779 and 1781) and by Price [116] when the second phase of the national population arguments heated up from 1779 (*qv*). Price quoted the actual figures of inhabitants for males and for females in the age ranges: under 2, 2 to 5, 5 to 10, 10 to 20, and by ten-year groups to 90 to 100. The number of inhabitants in Speen in Berkshire was taken in 1757 and later quoted by Price [117]. The 1757 listing for Douglas, Isle of Man has been mentioned above (see 1730).

Meanwhile, lists had been made in 1756 of Protestants in County Louth, Ireland who had taken an oath of allegiance or Commission of Array; the original lists are now in the NLI. In England, in the same year, the government had imposed a Silver Plate Tax which remained on the Statute Book until 1777. The returns for this, which include the names of the taxpayers and the amounts they paid, were deposited with the clerk to the county justices during the quarter sessions among which records they may be found today in county archives.

In 1757 it became necessary to introduce a new *Militia Act* as there were no competent persons left in the old county militia regiments to defend the local people in the event of an invasion, potentially by the French. All the professional soldiers were fighting on the continent in the relatively well organised armed forces established in 1660 as the new Standing Army. Those really interested in a military career had joined the army, leaving the old militia comprising only feeble amateurs. The 1757 Militia Act required that lists be made by counties in England and Wales of potential volunteers (men between 18 and 50) to serve in militia regiments. The clergy, teachers, apprentices, peace officers and peers were excluded. From the lists the actual recruits were picked by ballot; if they were unwilling or unable to serve they had to find a substitute - hence the initial lists have been termed Militia Ballot Lists, and the picked men appear on Militia Muster Rolls or Enrolment Lists.

By the mid 1760s annual Ballot Lists were being prepared in most counties, the system being organised by the Privy Council through the county Lords Lieutenant and their deputies and the parish constables. The lists were, accordingly, collected by parishes into hundreds or wapentakes (or in some cases especially created subdivisions); each hundred provided one Company for the county regiment of militia. Although not quarter sessions business, many county justices became involved in administering the balloting system and the lists are filed with quarter sessions records. In other instances the records remain among county lieutenancy papers or in some cases in private archives, see JSWG's *Militia Lists and Musters 1757-1876* [118]. Accepting that neither the Ballot Lists, the Muster Rolls nor the Enrolment Lists are censuses, and that several of the lists are far from complete, those that were carefully compiled do provide names of some of the men in certain localities between the ages of 18 and 50. A listing of able-bodied Protestants in eight parishes in County Cork, Ireland was compiled in 1757 and published in 1964 [119].

A dispute over mill rights in Manchester caused a census to be taken there in 1757. Whilst the population figure of 19,839 has survived, the original returns of this census do not appear to have done so. The existence of this census was referred to in the article 'Observations on the State of Population in Manchester and other adjacent Places', which was published in the *Philosophical Transactions of the Royal Society* during 1774 [120]; the "observations" were made by Dr Thomas Percival although they were "communicated" to the Royal Society by Price.

Names of Freeholders from 1758 to 1775 in Queen's County (Laois), Ireland were published by County Kildare Archaeological Society in 1915 (Vol VIII page 309).

A further *Militia Act* in 1758 required all males between 18 and 50 and their occupations to be listed; thus the listings for this year provides more names than did the previous year and further information on them as well. Some constables included the numbers of children under 10, or even their actual ages, in their lists. Incidentally in 1762, by yet another *Militia Act*, the age range was altered to 18 to 45.

Another Bill for vital statistics was placed before Parliament in 1758. Although no census as such was mentioned, this was another attempt to take account of the question of a rising or falling population and the realisation that there was a definite lack of official statistics on which to base any accurate discussion. Like Potter's 1753 *Population Bill*, the 1758 one also failed.

In 1760 a census was taken at West Wycombe, Buckinghamshire. The original return is at the county record office in Aylesbury.

Lists of Freeholders in 1761 of Limerick City and County, and of County Westmeath (these lists continue to 1788) may be consulted in the NLI.

The detailed results of a census taken in 1762 at Whitehaven, Cumberland have been deposited in Whitehaven Public Library. The properties in the town and the occupations of the inhabitants were included in the return.

In 1764 an ecclesiastical survey of Papists in the York Diocese was undertaken parish by parish. The results may be found in a manuscript book, now cared for by the Borthwick Institute and filed with the Bishopthorpe manuscripts.

Another Cumberland census was undertaken in 1765, in this year for the town of Maryport. The returns for Maryport, which include occupations, are among the Benson records at Cockermouth Castle. The proportions of natives and strangers were included in the survey taken at Stratford-upon-Avon in 1765, although the main purpose of this census appears to have been to identify those who had suffered from smallpox. The findings were recorded in 1806 by Robert Bell Wheler [121] in his *History and antiquities of Stratford upon Avon, comprising... .*

During this year the clergy in London and Westminster parishes were asked to supply information on Papists, such as their numbers, where they met and the names of any Popish priests who were encouraging people in Popery in their parishes. Similar questions were asked in the following year. The responses for 1765 and 1766 are today with the Fulham Palace Papers [122] held by the Church Commissioners. All Church of Ireland clergy were asked exactly the same questions in March and April 1766. The quality of their responses varies from comprehensive lists of all householders with names and addresses, to mere numerical summaries. Names were recorded on the lists for twenty of the Irish counties, in as many as 55 parishes in Tipperary and 47 parishes in Cork, but in only one parish each in Armagh and Waterford, and no names at all in parishes in Kerry and Kildare Counties. The original lists were lost in 1922 but many transcripts and abstracts had been made before this, nowadays conveniently listed in the reading room of the INA.

In 1767 a second survey (see 1757) for Ackworth, Yorkshire, was taken; on this occasion the numbers of houses - inhabited and uninhabited - were noted as well as the numbers of families and inhabitants. As in the case of the previous survey the 1767 results were referred to both by Price [123], who mentions a "curious register kept by Dr Lee", and by Wales. Lists of Freeholders for this year were compiled in Ireland for County Carlow and Dublin City; the former was published in *The Irish Genealogist* in 1980, the original list for the latter is in the INA. According to Hugh Calvert's *History of Hull* [124], an enumeration was taken here in 1767 with nearby Sculcoates indicating a combined population of 12,963.

Further lists of Papists were required in 1767, but this time on a national basis, parish by parish, as a result of a resolution from the House of Lords on 22 May 1767. Throughout the country the clergy were asked to supply names, sexes, ages, occupations and length of time resident in each parish. Some returns are comprehensive but for others only summaries have survived in the material now in the House of Lords Record Office. Some returns went to diocesan registries, and have been passed on to county record offices, and some are in Lambeth Palace Library. Supporting evidence in county Quarter Sessions records often shows individuals' names. Several returns and some Quarter Sessions data have been transcribed, published and indexed with commentaries by a variety of specialist groups [125].

For Newbury and adjoining Speen in Berkshire enumerations of the numbers of families and inhabitants were conducted in 1768. Although the whereabouts of the original returns are not now known, details of the survey were quoted by Price [126] and again a century later by Walter Money who gave figures for the districts in his *History of the ancient town... of... Newbury, Berks...* published in 1887.

In 1770 enumerations were undertaken in the Devon parish of Okeford; in Birmingham (it was then a town in Warwickshire), distinguishing numbers of males and females; in Corsham and in Steeple Ashton, Wiltshire; in Liverpool; and in Bury, Lancashire. The Okeford [127] figures of the numbers of inhabitants (422) and the Bury figures for houses and inhabitants were referred to by Price, whilst the Birmingham figures of the numbers of houses and inhabitants were quoted, not only by Price, but also in the *Tradesmen's True Guide or a Universal Directory for the Towns of Birmingham, Wolverhampton, Walsall and Dudley*, written in 1770 by Sketchley and Adam. The lists of names of the men and their occupations at Corsham and the inhabitants at Steeple Ashton have been deposited in the Wiltshire Record Office at Trowbridge. 1770 has already been mentioned (see 1700) as the last year during the eighteenth century when regular decennial enumerations were taken in Liverpool. The work of Dr Enfield on the population of Liverpool, apart from the commentaries of Price, and incidentally also of Howlett, is referred to below (see 1773).

At some time during this decade enumerations were conducted in Wiltshire at Calne, of families and inhabitants, and at nearby Bremhill, of houses and inhabitants. Whilst Price quoted [128] both of these, the present location of the original documentation is not known.

In 1771 at Swinderby, Lincolnshire the vicar, Dr Disney, took a census, naming all his parishioners but he sent only the figures to Price. This census is now in Lincolnshire Archives [129]. In the same year an enumeration was taken at Leeds, Yorkshire. Both sets of figures were quoted [130] by Price. The latter enumeration, together with another taken in 1775, was discussed at some length by F Beckwith in the 1948 publication of the Thoresby Society [131], comparing figures quoted earlier by Price and Wales. The work of Drs Lucas and Wood, analysing data in and around Leeds in the latter part of the eighteenth century was also discussed by Beckwith. In his *Observations* Price quoted figures for the total inhabitants in the town of Leeds, the total in the villages and country near the town and numbers of males, females, married persons, widows, widowers, unmarried males and unmarried females over 20 and girls and boys under 20. For 1775, a different breakdown of the figures was quoted in 1795 by Aikin in his book (on page 571) on Manchester (see 1781 below) who also added a gem of social history: "It is to be observed, that in the lowest rank of people there is often more than one family to a house".

On 1 January 1772 Rev Mr Travis, the vicar of Eastham, Cheshire and his uncle, the vicar of Royton, Lancashire, undertook "comprehensive censuses" (*sic*) in their respective parishes; the results of these were quoted by Dr Percival in his article [132] in *Philosophical Transactions* in the 1774 issue, where he also attempted to relate death and disease to rainfall in that area of England. In March that year an accurate account was made of the numbers of houses, inhabitants and lodgers in part of St Pancras, London and later referred to by Price [133], as was that also taken during the year of the numbers of families and inhabitants in the village of Aldwinckle [134], Northamptonshire. In July and August, also in 1772, exact surveys were taken respectively in Altrincham, Cheshire and in the parish of St Mary, Chester; both were discussed in the Royal Society's *Philosophical Transactions* for 1774, the former by Percival with the Eastham and Royton figures, the latter by Dr J Haygarth [135] who had taken the Chester survey himself anyway. Dr Haygarth's article, which also compared the Chester figures with those for Northampton, Norwich and London, was complemented by another [136] in 1778 concerning a subsequent survey of the whole of Chester which he undertook in 1774. Also in 1772, in August, a listing was made at Cuxham, Oxfordshire, of all those inhabitants who had contracted smallpox. Those who had been given the disease by inoculation were distinguished on the listing from those who had otherwise caught it. The names were originally entered in the parish marriage register which commenced in 1754, now deposited in the county record office in Oxford.

Many local surveys were conducted in 1773 as interest in population figures spread throughout the country. In some cases names, ages and addresses are given on the surviving records, in other cases only the results as numbers appear. Some were at the direct request of Price or Percival, who have already been mentioned, to provide them with data for their arguments which they subsequently published. Other censuses seem to have been taken for local interest or information only, but most likely were inspired by the public debate taking place. The Bolton (with the suburb of Little Bolton), Lancashire, survey of April 1773 and those in Derbyshire at Chinley, Brownside and Bugsworth taken in September by Rev Mr Harrison of Chapel en le Frith were definitely for Percival's research; and he personally undertook a census of the Manchester and Salford townships in the summer of that year, referring to the results in his 1774 article mentioned above. For these two townships Percival quoted the numbers of houses, families, males, females, married persons, widowers, widows, those under 15 and those above 50, the male lodgers, the female lodgers and the empty houses - in fact almost every conceivable piece of information apart from the names of individuals in all the various categories. He even concluded that for Manchester and Salford there were six and two-fifth persons per house and four and a quarter individuals in a family from the total population of 27,246 - the sort of data that could usefully be woven into a social or family history for that area and period. In the same article Percival also referred to a census of Bury, Lancashire "just executed" and he quoted the results of a 1773 enumeration at Monton in the same county. Rev Mr Bolton, who helped collect some of the statistics in Monton for Percival, commented in words not unique to the eighteenth century that "drunkenness is more destructive to mankind, than pleurisies, fevers or the most malignant distempers".

Price also quoted [137] numbers of houses and inhabitants for Bolton and Little Bolton in his *Observations* but he was able to add similar numbers for Chippenham, Wiltshire and for Liverpool, and for Manchester and Salford, adding only the numbers of families - not the full data of Percival. For Hale Chapel, Cheshire, Price was able to refer to Percival's figures of males, females, married persons, widowers, widows and the totals for inhabitants under 15 and over 50 and to similar data in Lancashire for Mr Evans's congregation at Horwich, Rev Mr Smalley's congregation at Darwen and Rev Mr Barker's congregation at Cockey Moor. For Rev Mr Mercer's congregation at Chowbent, Price quoted numbers of males, females, married persons, widowers, widows, males under 10, females under 10, males over 50 and females over 50. Aikin also quoted many 1773 figures for houses and inhabitants in the thirty to forty mile radius from Manchester in his 1795 book (see 1781).

Although "survey" is the term most frequently used by Price, and he occasionally referred to a "census", particularly for his work on population during this decade little, if any, of the original documentation can now be found; this suggests that many of the figures were calculated from parish register entries rather than from house to house enquiries. However, the occasional reference to "a very accurate survey" or to one taken "with much labour" does indicate that a more rigorous census had been made, and hence the search today for the original documentation, possibly bearing names and further details on individuals, is worthy of consideration.

Dr John Aikin was responsible for analysing the Bill of Mortality for Warrington, Lancashire for 1773, the results of which were published in *Philosophical Transactions* [138]; in that article Aikin argued that as Warrington had 1,600 to 1,700 houses and with five persons per house the number of inhabitants was "somewhat above 8,000". Aikin also referred to the figures, but with no commentary, in his 1795 book on Manchester (see below under 1781). A Blandford Forum, Dorset, survey was obviously a direct result of the *Philosophical Transactions'* publicity, because details of the results from Blandford, which included an estimate of births to Dissenters, were discussed by Dr Richard Pulteney in his article [139] which was published on its pages in 1778.

On the other hand, the surveys of the populations of Bewdley, Wribbenhall and Kidderminster in Worcestershire were publicised by Treadway Russell Nash in his *Collections for the history of Worcestershire*, published between 1781 and 1799 [140]. The 1773 enumeration of Liverpool was taken by Dr William Enfield, the results of which he published in 1774 with those taken every ten years from 1700 to 1770, in the second edition of his ... *history of Liverpool* ... [141], referred to above in conjunction with the 1700 enumeration. The figures were reproduced in *Philosophical Transactions* [142] with a commentary on the huge increase in the population of "Leverpool" from 5,714 to 34,004 during those seventy years.

A 1773 enumeration taken by the vicar of St Laurence, Ramsgate, Kent, and those which the same vicar took in 1785 and 1792, were referred to by William Boys in his *Collections for an History of Sandwich in Kent....* published in 1792, and by Edward Hastead in his *History and topographical survey of the County of Kent* in 1801 [143]. In June 1773 John Becher drew up "an accurate review of all the families in Renhold" in Bedfordshire with a "comprehensive account of their several characters which were searched into with indefatigable industry". This fascinating local census can be studied in the county archives [144] at Bedford.

On 17 April 1774 Colerne, Wiltshire was struck by a severe fire. A list was drawn up of the poor sufferers, their ages, their occupations and the value of their property. Although not a complete census, a list such as this, now in the record office at Trowbridge, may be of more value to a social or family historian than an unemotional survey or mere enumeration.

Price and Percival were almost as active in 1774 as in the previous year. Population figures of families and inhabitants for High Wycombe, Buckinghamshire were quoted by Price [145], and the *Gentleman's Magazine* for 1800 [146] published a report of the 1774 "very accurate account" of the inhabitants which was being taken at the request of Dr Price; however, the original document appears to have been lost. The local enumeration of the numbers of houses and inhabitants at Eastry, Kent is also quoted by Price [147]. Haygarth took a personal interest (Price stated that the survey was "made with great care under the direction of Dr Haygarth") in the population figures for the parishes including the suburbs of Chester in 1774 (see 1772, above); Haygarth's figures included families, inhabitants, males, females, married persons, widowers, widows, those under 15 and those over 50, numbers who "had recovered of, and those who had died of, the small pox" in 1774, and those who were ill of the "small pox" and those who had not had it in January 1775. Percival personally saw to the taking of an enumeration for the parish and the thirty-one townships for the whole of Manchester (as a sequel to his work of the previous year). The originals of the Manchester surveys are deposited in the library of Chetham College at Manchester University. Percival's commentary on these was published in *Philosophical Transactions* for 1774 and 1775 [148]. Towards the end of his article in the latter year Percival quoted the numbers of males and of females in the townships of Manchester and Salford, in the parish of Manchester, in Bolton, Little Bolton, Monton, Hale, Horwich, Darwen, Cockey (Moor) (near Bolton), Chowbent, Ackworth, Eastham, Chinley, Brownside and Bugsworth. He also identified numbers of widowers and widows in the parish of Manchester and Salford, in the townships of each of these, and in Monton, Hale, Horwich, Darwen, Cockey, Chowbent, Chinley, and Brownside and Bugsworth.

Later in the 1775 volume of *Philosophical Transactions* [149], in an article on 'Observations on the Difference between the Duration of Human Life in Towns and in Country Parishes and Villages', the names are given of several vicars who provided Price with data for that article; among the data are further population figures for other places, presumably taken in 1774 or before, although dates are not stated. Price duplicated the publication of some of these details in his own *Observations*. In yet another article [150] in *Philosophical Transactions*, (in 1776) Percival referred to the August 1774 parish survey of Tattenhall, Cheshire, taken by its curate, and to the survey taken in the same month by the incumbent at Waverton, also in Cheshire. Price elaborated [151] slightly in his *Observations* by stating that the survey of these two parishes provided numbers of males, females and the total population above the age of 14. Price additionally quoted an enumeration of the families and inhabitants in Bala, Wales also undertaken in 1774.

6. Eighteenth century listings: 1775 to 1787

1775 saw the conducting of at least six local enumerations: that at Leeds, Yorkshire has already been referred to (see 1771). The results from Ashton under Lyne, Lancashire were quoted by Aikin in his 1795 book (p 228) on Manchester (see 1781 below), by Percival in his 1776 article (*qv*), and by Price who broke the results down into: total population, males, females, total married, those under 5, 5 to 10, 10 to 20, 20 to 50, 50 to 70 and 70 to 90. That at Beaminster, Dorset was taken in conjunction with the parish rates and the original can be consulted at the Dorset Record Office at Dorchester. At Cirencester, Gloucestershire an exact count of the population for that year was published in Rudder's work on Gloucestershire (see the Stroud survey for 1756). The Corporation of Salisbury, Wiltshire was responsible for taking the census in that city in 1775 which included the relative numbers of strangers to natives; the results of this survey were included in *Salisbury* by R Benson and H Hatcher, published in 1883. At Sandford in Devon, 1775 was the first of five years (the others were 1783, 1790, 1793 and 1800) when censuses with names of individuals were recorded. The originals are now in the Devon Record Office at Exeter with other Sandford parish records. In addition, during 1775, names of landowners in County Kilkenny, Ireland and of gentry in County Waterford were identified and listed, the latter published in 1913 [152].

Evidently there was only one local survey undertaken in 1776, the year of the American Revolution, and that was at Sandwich, Kent. This did not escape Price's beady eye, however, and he referred [153] to it, quoting Boys' work (see 1773) which included the numbers of houses and persons in the town incorporating those in three workhouses and two hospitals. There are, furthermore, for this year, surviving list of names of voters in Ireland for the counties of Antrim (in the PRONI), and for Limerick and Tipperary (in the INA). A listing of Freemen of County Wexford for 1776 was published in *The Irish Genealogist* in 1974 and 1976 [154].

In 1777 a national tax was introduced on Male Servants whereby households employing them had to pay the levy. It was, accordingly, not a census as such and in the majority of cases the servants are not named although the households are clearly identified; but it does enable comparisons to be made nationally, in contrast to the profusion of local surveys being conducted in this decade. A most complex scale of charges was applied depending on whether the servant was married or single, whether he was employed as a book-keeper, steward, warehouseman, waiter, groom, or stable-keeper, and whether he was let for hire, if in livery or not. Servants engaged in husbandry, manufacture or any trade were exempt as were those employed by the Royal Family or those in service at Oxford or Cambridge Universities or at the public schools of Westminster, Eton and Winchester. Male servants at some hospitals and those of naval or army personnel below officer rank were also exempt. Army or naval officers who were disabled or who were on half-pay were additionally exempt. This tax remained in force until 1852. The Society of Genealogists holds the returns for 1780 which give the names of 24,750 people paying this tax on 50,000 un-named servants.

There appear to have been special surveys in 1777 of houses, and in some cases of inhabitants, on which Price believed reliance could be placed; those in Suffolk which he particularly mentioned [155] were Beccles, Bungay, Henham, Sollerton, Shipmeadow, Weston, Wenbaston, Southwold, Aldeburgh, Orford and Gorlestone; Price also quoted figures collected by Wales for Westhall, Wangford, Holton, Spexhall, Swilland, Tuddenham, Westerfield, Wisset, Witnesham, Blythford and Bramfield in Suffolk and Ashill, Clapton, Ilminster and Wayford in Somersetshire. There was an accurate survey, under the direction of Dr Bisset, of houses and inhabitants at Skelton in Yorkshire, quoted by Price [156] and the exact survey for Evesham was quoted in Nash's work on Worcestershire [157] (see the 1773 surveys which were undertaken in Worcestershire). A Maidstone, Kent survey was quoted by Price [158] in his debate on the differences between cottages and houses. Figures also for London, Thaxted, Essex, two other (unnamed) parishes in Essex and one (also unnamed) in Kent and for Northampton, Chester and Shrewsbury in 1777 were also used by Price in his arguments - again quoting from returns of window tax surveyors or other special surveys. A Freeholders' Register for 1777 and also for the years 1780 to 1795, for County Down, Ireland, is in the PRONI. An article on some Protestant inhabitants of Carrickmacross, County Monaghan, Ireland in 1777 was published in Vol VI, No 1 of the *Clogher Record* in 1966.

In 1778 a survey of the houses and population of the Bedfordshire parish Podington and its hamlet of Hinwick was undertaken, the results of which were communicated in 1782 by the vicar, Oliver St John Cooper, to John Nicholls who incorporated them into his *Collections towards the History and Antiquities of Bedfordshire.* Cooper became vicar of Thurleigh in 1784 and in 1788 undertook a similar survey there, and also another for Podington (and separately for Hinwick) and yet another for his neighbouring birthplace, Milton Ernest. The originals of the 1788 surveys which include surnames and some Christian names are in the British Library (Add. Ms. 34383 pp 43-45); they were transcribed by the contemporary County Archivist, Chris Pickford, and published in 1987 [159]. The numbers of families and inhabitants in Worsley, Parton, Pendleton, Pendlebury and Clifton (all in Lancashire) in 1778 were quoted by Price [160] in his *Observations*. An interesting contemporary list of the inhabitants of Waterford City, Ireland was published in *Freeman's Journal*, a Dublin Newspaper, in two successive issues on 29 October and 5 November 1778. A list of Roman Catholic merchants, traders and manufacturers in Dublin for the years 1778 to 1782 was published, in 1960, in *Reportorium Novum*, the Dublin Diocesan Historical Record.

Examples of censuses that were taken in Scotland on particular estates for specific purposes are those of 1779 and 1792 [161] for the Duke of Argyll in Kintyre.

Although the former year was really an enumeration of tenants on the estates on mainland and insular Argyll, for each farm the listing does provide the number of resident families, the numbers of tacksmen, tacksmen's sons, the servants and cottars, but not the total population for each farm; a transcript of the 1779 listing was prepared by E R Cregreen of the Extra-mural Department of Glasgow University. The listing for 1792 is more valuable for family historians as it gives the total population on each farm by name and age. A useful commentary on how these censuses can be used to analyse the areas of settlement, range of ages and social status was written by Alan Gailey [162] from the Department of Geography at Glasgow University in 1960.

A survey of houses, families and inhabitants, as a result of a most unusual situation was conducted in Nottingham in September 1779: a party of unnamed gentlemen became involved in a wager causing a public subscription to be raised to pay for this survey to be undertaken. The results were published by Robert Lowe of Oxton in 1798 in an appendix to the second edition of his *General View of the Agriculture of the County of Nottingham* [163]. The Rev Mr Wilson, vicar of Biddulph, Staffordshire undertook an accurate survey of the families and inhabitants by males and females within his parish in April 1779; his original survey, which names the householders, is in the County Record Office [164]. Wilson sent the figures from his survey to Dr Haygarth at Chester and they were also quoted by Price [165]. Additionally in that year G Young [166] gave details of the numbers of houses and inhabitants of Worcester in his *Plan· of the City and Suburbs of Worcester.* 1779 was memorable in Wembworthy, Devon, as a census of the population with their ages, was also undertaken there that year; the returns are now in the Devon Record Office in Exeter [167].

It was during 1779 that Rev Richard Price added further fuel to the population debate by publishing his *Essay on the Population of England and Wales*, initially as an appendix to *The Doctrine of Annuities and Assurances on Lives and Survivorships* written by his nephew, William Morgan, the actuary to the Equitable Assurances Society. Hidden at the end of Morgan's learned work, Price's essay, which concluded that the population of the country taken as a whole was falling, did not make an immediate impact; but the following year Price published his essay separately and the public argument burst into flame.

William Eden, first Lord Auckland, and a well respected public figure and politician, criticised Price straight away in a new edition of his *Four Letters to the Earl of Carlisle* which he produced the same year. During the subsequent year, 1781, William Wales, a mathematics teacher at Christ's Hospital, London and an astronomer who had accompanied Cook on his Pacific voyages, produced *An Inquiry into the Present State of Population in England and Wales* and Rev John Howlett, vicar of Great Badow, and concurrently also of Dunmow in Essex, published *An Examination of Dr Price's Essay on the Population of England and Wales.* Howlett concluded that the population was rising, in stark contrast to Price's thesis.

Price was, however, ready to fight off his critics. He had a strong personality and was a forceful Presbyterian preacher, well-loved and respected not only by his London congregations but also by those who read his literary contributions to eighteenth century society. And so Price's *Essay* went into another edition in 1780 with an appendix to answer his critics. Further editions of his *Essay*, and also of his earlier work *Observations on Reversionary Payments*, were used in the counter-attack. As discussed above it is obvious that not a few of the locally conducted surveys were taken at the request of Price or one of his opponents to glean evidence on the pop-ulation figures for one side or the other of the ensuing discussions.

Land tax in some shape or form had been applied since 1692 and remained viable until 1831, but in 1780 the arrangements for its administration were changed. From this year the assessment returns had to be sent to the Clerk of the Peace for the immediate county at the Spring Quarter Sessions. Thus from 1780 the original returns, where they survive, are with the Quarter Sessions records in county record offices. There is, additionally, an almost complete set of returns covering the whole country, but only for the year 1798, now in the PRO [168]. The documents for this particular year have probably survived because from 1798 land owners were able to make a once-off payment to enable them to be exonerated from further liability to pay the annual tax, and it was necessary to have a complete national listing of land owners and occupiers. As mentioned above, prior to 1780 these returns may be found in a variety of archive depositories. The tax was assessed on the real estate and personalty of persons owning land having an annual value of above twenty shillings, and also on certain public salaries and pensions. Thus poorer people were exempt and were not included on the lists. The assessment system was supervised by county commissioners, who appointed parish assessors and collectors. Tenants also paid this tax but they deducted it from their rents; thus most assessment lists bear the names of landlords and tenants. The amount paid, which should have been calculated at the rate of four shillings in the pound, was shown on the returns alongside the names of the owners and occupiers of the houses and land. This data is useful to the social and family historian to give an indication of the economic status of a named individual. Several of these land tax assessment lists have been transcribed and published by local historical, antiquarian, and archaeological societies.

An enumeration at Farnham, Surrey undertaken in 1780 was referred to during the following year by William Wales [169] in his *Inquiry*. The original documents of the Farnham survey have not been traced, nor have those of the "exact survey" of houses in Christleton, Lancashire (*sic*), referred to by Price [170]. A list of Free-holders in Co Roscommon, Ireland for 1780 is in the Irish Genealogical Office.

In 1780, again on a national basis (see 1767), lists of Papists were made parish by parish. These were in response to an address from the House of Lords on 3 July 1780. Although not demanded by the Archbishops of Canterbury and York, many returns include names, ages, sexes, occupations and the length of time resident in the parish. Some returns give initials rather than names, thus providing the Catholic researcher with an interesting challenge. Many originals are in the House of Lords Record Office [171] but the results have been listed in the *Journal of the House of Lords* [172]. The parish returns for the London Diocese are held by the Catholic Record Society [173] and some incumbents' original returns, formerly in diocesan registries, are now in county record offices.

In 1781 Dr Aikin obtained another enumeration of the houses and inhabitants of the town and township of Warrington, including Poulton, Fearnhead and Woolston, (see 1773), the results of which he included in *A description of the country from thirty to forty miles round Manchester; containing...*, published in 1795. This survey was mentioned by Price as providing numbers of inhabitants and houses, inhabited and uninhabited, as were two of Maidstone, Kent [174] one of houses, families and inhabitants taken the same year and another the next year, 1782 (*qv*). Two surveys were taken in Wiltshire in 1781, one at Swindon, the other at Warminster. The former [175] was quoted by Price, the latter [176] in the 1965 edition of the *Victoria County History of Wiltshire*, but the whereabouts of the originals of both these surveys are now unknown.

The 'General Account of the number of persons in each house' in the village of Cardington, Bedfordshire was taken on 1 January 1782, probably by the school-master, James Lilburne. The original returns, which name every inhabitant, their ages, relationships in each house, occupations and other details, are in the county record office in Bedford. However, a most comprehensive annotated transcript was prepared by David Baker and published by the Bedfordshire Historical Record Society in 1973, as mentioned in the Preface to this Cameo. Also in Bedfordshire, Rev Richard How of Aspley Guise entered into correspondence with John Howlett in Essex regarding the population of Aspley. How examined his parish registers from 1563 and the Poor Law expenditure within the parish. The original correspondence has been deposited in the local county archives [177], but was also quoted by Baker in his work on the detailed census of Cardington.

Additionally in January 1782 a second survey of Belfast (see 1757) indicated the numbers of houses, numbers of inhabitants, male and female, the number of looms and the number of houses selling beer and spirits. Price referred to this survey in his *Observations* [178]. A listing of persons in Cudolf, County Donegal, Ireland in 1782 was reproduced in Amy Young's *300 Years in Inishowen*, published in 1929.

The September 1782 survey of Maidstone, Kent, referred to by Price with that of the year before, was published in 1782 as a pamphlet *Observations on the Increas-ed Population, Healthiness, etc of the Town of Maidstone*. However, the author's name was not published and whilst Price attributed this census to John Howlett, the Essex vicar mentioned above, it was also attributed to the curate of Maidstone, Rev J Deane, by J M Russell in his *History of Maidstone....* published in 1881. The original pamphlet kept at Maidstone Museum details the numbers of families, houses and male and female inhabitants; male servants, female servants, women above 70, men above 70, girls under 15 and boys under 15 were separately enumerated in the town and in the country.

In the Autumn of 1782 "a very accurate survey" was made of the inhabited and uninhabited houses in Birmingham; but only their numbers, not their occupants or owners, appear to have survived. These numbers are quoted by Price [179]. Dr William White undertook a survey of York as a contribution to the population debate, publishing [180] his interpretation of the results in *Philosophical Transactions* in 1782.

The Minehead, Somerset, survey of 1783, similarly to that of 1705 (*qv*), was referred to in 1791 by John Collinson in his *History....of Somerset*. The Sandford, Devon census of 1783 has been mentioned (see 1775). A listing of Freemen and Freeholders of 1783 for Cork City, Ireland is in the NLI.

In 1784 a tax on horses, mares, geldings and mules, whether used for riding (including racing) or as post horses, or for drawing carriages or in husbandry, was levied nationally. The levy varied enormously depending on the uses to which the horses were put, pleasure horses being taxed at considerably higher rates than husbandry horses. A butcher using a horse when carrying out his trade had to pay the same high rate as for a racehorse, whereas a bailiff in using a horse in his work paid a slightly lower rate. The duty on horses above thirteen hands high was greater than on smaller horses. There were certain exemptions: "horses drawing any carriage not liable to duty, or carrying burdens in the course of trade or occupation of the person to whom such horse shall belong, if rode only when going for a load, or· returning, or going for medical assistance, or to or from any market, or place of public worship, election of members of parliament; or to or from any court of justice, or to or from any meeting of commissioners of taxes". All this meant that anyone possessing horses had to pay the sum annually (unless the exemptions could be applied), with the result that the taxation lists, which for most counties are filed with the quarter sessions records, provide useful sources of names and enable more pictorial inform-ation to be added to a family or social history. This tax was increased in 1808 and 1822 and remained on the statute books until 1874; husbandry horses were totally exempt from this duty from 1822.

Another national levy imposed in 1784 was the Game Duty Tax. All persons who wished to kill or even to sell game - and for the purposes of this tax woodcock, snipe, quail, landrail and coney were also included - were obliged to have licences. These were issued annually, taking effect from 6 April each year, in every county by the Clerks of the Peace in exchange for a monetary payment. Manorial game-keepers were not exempted from this levy, which demonstrates the further decline of the influence of ancient manorial rights and the rising importance of county administration. Nevertheless there were exemptions for those who caught woodcocks or snipes with nets or springs, or those who caught coneys in warrens or enclosed grounds; furthermore, no tax was payable by persons who caught game on their own land with ferrets or nets. This Game Duty Tax remained in force until 1807. The lists of those who paid were filed with the quarter sessions records within each county.

A survey of Lancaster was taken by Thomas Batty, the parish clerk, in 1784. A statistical analysis is now in the corporation archives; Batty's work was publicised by C Clark in 1807 when he reproduced the data in *An Historical and Descriptive Account of the Town of Lancaster*. The 1784 survey of Douglas, Isle of Man was referred to under 1730. "An accurate account" of the population of Great Yarmouth, Norfolk during 1784 was referred to in his *Notices of Great Yarmouth* by J H Drury, published in 1826; the original account has not been located. Also in 1784 enumerations were undertaken in Westmorland of Kendal, Burton in Kendal, Kirky Lonsdale, and in Sedbergh; the original documents appear not to have survived although the results were published in *Local Chronology* in 1865 and Sir Frederick Morton Eden referred to the Kendal figures in his *State of the Poor* [181] which was published in 1797. Sir Frederick, a nephew of William Eden (see 1779), was particularly interested in life expectancy rates and the type of information which could be predicted from Bills of Mortality - in fact he was one of the founders and subsequently Chairman of the Globe Insurance Company.

A tax was imposed on a nation-wide basis in 1785 on all households employing female servants, similar to that imposed on male servants in 1777 (*qv*). The Female Servants' Tax, sometimes referred to as the Maid Servants' Tax, remained in force until 1792.

Locally in 1785 an enumeration of the numbers of families and souls was undertaken in Leicester. The results were quoted in 1791 by John Throsby in his *History and antiquities of....Leicester*, but no original documents survive. A detailed census undertaken for Frome, Somerset, which was referred to by both Collinson [182] and Eden [183] is now in private hands, but there are copies at Somerset Record office and Frome Museum. The census names the householders and their occupations and lists the numbers of males and females in each house. With future historical researchers obviously in mind the census names the owner of every house, the number of scribblers and shearmen in each, the numbers of looms owned by weavers, and the number of cows kept by each householder.

A list of the inhabitants of the Wiltshire parish of Little Cheverall, also taken during 1785, may be consulted at the county record office in Trowbridge. The Ramsgate, Kent census undertaken by the vicar in 1785 (and 1792) has already been mentioned (see 1773). A series of deeds from 1785 to 1879 relating to Kilkenny City, Ireland includes several lists of the inhabitants, and so provide some useful census-type listings; these are mentioned in the Kilkenny Archaeological Society Journal, *Old Kilkenny Review*, in 1982 (Vol 2 No 4). Also beginning in 1785 is a series of Rent Rolls for Westport, County Mayo, Ireland which continue until 1815; details of these were published in *Cathair ne Mart* in 1982 (Vol 2 No 1).

An account of Cess-payers in six parishes in County Louth, Ireland from 1786 to 1792, transcribed by Rev Chancellor J B Leslie from a Vestry Minute Book, was published in the *County Louth Archaeological Society Journal* in 1937 (Vol 9 No 1 pages 42-45).

A list of the inhabitants of Chisleden, Wiltshire, was made on 15 February 1787; the original list is in the Wiltshire County Record Office at Trowbridge. At quarter sessions in both Cumberland and Westmorland in 1787 all parishes were asked to conduct a local census and forward the returns to the Clerks of the Peace. The majority of the original documents for Westmorland parishes has been deposited in the county archives at Kendal with the quarter sessions records - but for Cumberland enumerations only for Carlisle appear to have survived. Also for Carlisle are the *Observations on the Bills of Mortality* published annually by J Heysham from 1779 to 1787, the last year containing the figures requested by the quarter sessions. The original observations from 1781 to 1787 are housed in the public library at Carlisle, but were summarized by both Henry Lonsdale [184] and William Hutchinson [185] later in the eighteenth century.

7. Listings from 1788

On 1 April 1788 the States Parliament on Jersey, in response to a request from the English Parliament, ordered a survey of the island. The instructions were to list the numbers of men, women and children both present and absent; however, the authorities in the parish of St Lawrence interpreted the ordinance further and on 9 April 1788 made lists of the names of all the parishioners with their ages, by *vingtaines* (sub-divisions of parishes). These lists are extremely useful to family historians, as with many Jersey records, because wives are listed with their maiden surnames. For the other parishes only population numbers appear to have been taken. The original returns are in La Société Jersiaise Library, but transcripts of the St Lawrence lists were published by the Channel Islands Family History Society [186] in 1980, 1981 and 1982.

During 1788 James Pilkington was active in Derbyshire, either conducting or initiating surveys in at least twenty-one parishes in the county. In the second edition of his *A View of the Present State of Derbyshire with an account of its most remarkable antiquities...*, published in 1803, Pilkington quoted the "exact enumeration" of Chesterfield [187], taken in December 1788 and the "actual enumeration" of Derby - which he took personally during 1788. Statistical analyses of many other parishes were also included in the same work. Dr Percival, who had promoted the taking of enumerations in and around Manchester since the early 1770s (*qv*), took a further survey of Manchester township in 1788. The results of that survey were published as an appendix to his *Essays, Medical, Philosophical and Experimental* when it was reprinted in 1807. The figures for an enumeration of 1788 for the parish of Harrington, Cumberland, were incorporated in the Visitation Returns of 1788-9 of the Chester diocese. The original returns are in Cheshire Record Office. A Poll Book of 1788 for County Fermanagh, Ireland is in the PRONI.

In October 1789 an accurate count of Burton upon Trent, Staffordshire, was made, according to the *History and Antiquities of Staffordshire, ...including Erdeswick's Survey...* by Stebbing Shaw [188]; however, the original documents cannot now be traced. A similar situation pertains for the originals of the enumeration taken of Bolton, Lancashire during 1789 which was referred to by Aikin (see 1781). A list of voters in County Down, Ireland for 1789 is in the Deputy Court Cheque Book in the PRONI, whereas a list of Protestant Householders in Ferns, County Wexford, Ireland was published in *The Irish Ancestor*, Vol 13 No 2, 1981.

Between 1789 and 1793 the population figures for many Nottinghamshire parishes were obtained by going from house to house. The figures were quoted by Lowe [189] in his *General View...*, referred to above, in conjunction with the 1779 survey of Nottingham. It is believed that another census of Nottingham was taken in 1793;

according to Lowe the expenses incurred to undertake it were certainly paid for by Sir Richard Sutton, although the returns themselves appear to be missing today. However, a census for West Retford taken in 1794 has survived and is in the county archives.

In the Devon parishes of Sandford and Tiverton censuses were undertaken in 1790. The original returns of the former have been mentioned above (see 1775). For the latter an enumeration only was made in January of that year and quoted by Martin Dunsford in his *Historical Memoirs of the town and parish of Tiverton....* [190]. Lists of Freeholders in Ireland for this year survive for the Locale barony in County Down (the lists are in the PRONI), and for counties Longford and Roscommon (the lists are in the NLI); for the latter county the lists continue annually until 1799. A census of Corfe Castle for 1790 which included names, ages, conditions (married, bachelor etc), occupations and probable weekly incomes and paid by whom, was referred to [191] by Rev John Hutchins the rector of Wareham in his work on Dorset. This census also recorded, by sex, the housekeepers, children and grand-children resident with their parents, lodgers and inmates, servants and apprentices, and their addresses and names, ages and occupations.

In October 1790 at Hayes, Kent a list of the parishioners, household-by-household, was compiled by Rev John Till, the rector. Several households include the names of lodgers who do not appear in the parish registers, and the occupations of many of the individuals are given. This list, which was formerly among Till's papers in the Kent County Archives, is now housed [192] at Bromley Reference Library in Kent. Also during 1790 Dr Joshua Toulmin went from house to house in Taunton, Somerset to collect data on the population which he published both in his own *History of Taunton in the county of Somersetshire* [193] and also as an article [194] in the *Monthly Magazine and British Register*, a London-based periodical. Toulmin's separate *History....* was later enlarged by J Savage and G Webb and re-printed in 1874.

At Swinderby, Lincolnshire, a similar census to that of 1771 (*qv*) was undertaken in 1791; the original returns are in the county archives [195]. An account of a 1791 survey of Loughrea, County Galway, Ireland, which includes names of occupiers, was published in Vol 23 No 3 of the *Journal of the Galway Historical and Arch-aeological Society*. Lists of Freeholders in County Leitrim, and Landholders in Dromiskin, County Louth, also for 1791, are available - the former in the Geneal-ogical Office, Dublin, the latter appearing in J B Leslie's *History of Kilsaran Union of Parishes*, published in 1908.

The 1792 survey of Ramsgate, Kent has already been referred to above (see 1773 and 1785). At Kingston upon Hull, Yorkshire a census was taken during 1792 by the Society for Literary Information. This was referred to by J Ticknell in his *History of the Town and County of Kingston upon Hull* [196], published in 1796, and also by Eden [197]; H Clavert compares the 1792 figures with those for 1767 and 1777 in his *History of Hull* (see 1767). The Gentlemen, Farmers and inhabitants of Rugby (1,553 of them) signed a Declaration of attachment to the King and Constitution in 1792. The original is in Warwickshire Record Office [198]. *The Irish Ancestor* published [199] three lists of names for 1792: Protestants in Mohill barony, County Leitrim, leading Catholics in County Waterford, and Protestant householders in Ballycanew and Killtrisk, County Wexford. Also for 1792 is a valuation list (continuing to 1796) of corn tithes for Newcastle, County Wicklow, the original of which, containing names of the tenants, is in the NLI.

A nation-wide tax was imposed in 1793 on all holders of armorial bearings and remained in force until 1882. The tax was assessed at three levels: those who had a carriage had to pay more than those who did not, presumably because the achievement was seen by a wider audience by virtue of being displayed on the carriage. Those who also paid house duties, but who did not have a carriage, paid a lower tax than those who had a carriage - but they paid a higher tax than those who had neither carriage nor the obligation to pay house duties. The Armorial Bearings Tax was payable to the Clerk to the County Justices and the lists of those who paid and the amounts were filed with the quarter sessions records for the relevant county.

A locally conducted census of the Essex parish of Bocking in 1793 may be consulted at the county record office in Chelmsford. The Kendal survey for this year appears to have been taken under similar circumstances as that for 1784 (*qv*). It is quoted by Eden [200], but the original returns do not appear to have survived. The Sandford, Devon census was referred to above (see 1775). Militia records for County Armagh, Ireland from 1793 to 1808 are in Armagh County Library. A listing of Householders in 1793 of St Anne's parish, Shadon, County Cork, Ireland was published by the Cork Historical and Archaeological Society in 1942 [201]. A list of Protestants in Castlemack, County Dublin for this year is held in the Genealogical Office, Dublin, while a list of the residents of Newcastle, County Limerick, Ireland was published in *The Irish Ancestor* in 1984 [202].

In 1794 local surveys were conducted at Cambridge, Stockton upon Tees in Durham, West Retford in Nottinghamshire (see 1789), Brighton in Sussex and Skipton in Yorkshire. The Cambridge population figures may be found with the Bowtell Manuscripts at Downing College, Cambridge, with those for 1749 (*qv*). Reference to the Stockton census was made in Rev John Brewster's *Parochial History and Antiquities of Stockton upon Tees....* [203] published in 1829 although the original documents appear to have been lost; Brewster was rector of Egglescliffe. The Brighton survey was conducted prior to an inoculation campaign in the town and was referred to by Charles Wright [204] in *The Brighton Ambulator....* in 1818 as being "an exact enumeration". The Skipton census recorded 2,096 inhabitants in the town and identified the numbers of families as well; the whereabouts of the original returns are now unknown. A list of Roman Catholic Freemen in Galway town, Ireland in 1794 was published by the Galway Historical and Archaeological

Society [205], while a series of Militia Pay Lists and Muster Rolls from 1794 to 1799 for County Fermanagh, Ireland is in the PRONI.

A national duty on the use of Hair Powder was introduced on 5 May 1795; the powder itself was already the subject of a tax from an earlier law. Each individual who used hair powder was required to pay a guinea and in return received an annual licence although payment for two unmarried daughters exempted the rest of the household from the dues. Clergymen of any denomination who had an annual income of less than £100 were exempt from paying this tax, as were ranks below officer in the navy, army or militia, and members of the Royal Family and their servants. A gentleman was able to take out a licence for his butler, coachman, footman etc and if he changed them during the year, the licence stood good for the newly engaged servants. About 200,000 people paid this tax in the first year which encouraged Pitt, who had introduced the Bill, to have it raised to £1 3s 6d per head. There was, however, opposition to the principle of this levy causing cropping and combing out of the hair to become fashionable. The Duke of Bedford was foremost in leading this fashion, followed swiftly by many of the gentry, and then lower strata of society, initially in Bedfordshire. By 1869 only about £1,000 per annum was raised from approximately 800 individuals paying this duty and thus it was repealed that year.

In July 1795 a census, household by household, was conducted in the parish of St Andrew, Worcester - sometimes termed the "Tanners' and Glovers' parish". The original returns are in the county record office in Worcester.

A survey of the houses and inhabitants at Uley in Gloucestershire was undertaken in about 1795 by Michael Lloyd-Baker's great grandfather; he made a rough plan of the village in his estate pocket book and allocated a number to each of the 299 houses. Against every number, on a separate schedule, he listed both Christian and surnames of the occupants. When Michael Lloyd-Baker wrote *The Story of Uley* around 1910 he reproduced [206], in later editions but not the first, the sketch map and the associated list of names so enabling us to discover not only who was in the village but exactly where they all lived. Also in 1795 a detailed survey, including occupations, was conducted in Epsom, Surrey; the results without names were published in some depth by Eden [207].

In 1796 John Rickman wrote a memorandum on behalf of George Rose, the MP for Christchurch, Hampshire, on the potential advantages of conducting a general enumeration of the people in the British overseas possessions. This was sent to Charles Abbot, the MP for Helston, Cornwall. This event, in itself, may not appear particularly significant - there had, after all, been many similar suggestions over the years. But it should be noted that when Abbot later became Chief Secretary and Privy Seal in Ireland he chose Rickman as his secretary, and four years later Abbot and Rickman achieved what scores of other advocates of a national census had failed to do when Parliament accepted their proposals.

A Dog Tax, applicable on a national basis, was introduced during 1796 and remained in force until 1882. When first administered this tax was quite complicated because of the sliding scales related to the breed of dog and the purpose for which it was kept. Greyhounds, for example, were taxed at a higher rate than spaniels, lurchers or terriers, and other breeds were at a lower rate still. Whelps under six months were exempt. A pack of fox hounds could be taxed collectively. A licence was issued in return for the annual tax paid and fines were payable for those who failed to purchase a licence.

In an attempt to improve the Irish linen industry in 1796, the government gave a spinning wheel or loom to every person in Ireland who planted a certain amount of flax. For the counties of Armagh, Donegal, Down, Londonderry, Longford, Louth, Mayo, Meath, Monaghan, Roscommon and Tyrone, the names and parishes of over 3,000 persons in each county can be found in the Spinning Wheel Entitlement Lists - in fact for only Counties Dublin and Wicklow are there no entries at all. Altogether some 53,000 separate names are on these lists, now in the INA; microfiche surname indexes were published by All-Ireland Heritage Inc. in 1986, and these are also available in the INA and the PRONI.

In Carlisle in 1796 a further survey was conducted (see 1787). The results were published by Hutchinson in 1796 with those for 1781 to 1787 as mentioned above. A Freeholders' list for County Fermanagh, Ireland from 1796 to 1802 is in PRONI.

In 1797 at Harlow in Essex a census was undertaken locally, the original returns of which have been deposited in the Essex Record Office at Chelmsford. Two series of Yeomanry Muster Rolls, for County Fermanagh for 1797, and for County Londonderry from 1797 to 1804, are in the PRONI. A 1797 listing of the "chief" Roman Catholic inhabitants of Graiguenamanagh and Knocktopher, County Kilkenny, Ireland who had signed a declaration of loyalty, published in *Finn's Leinster Journal* on 22-25 November and on 2-6 December 1797, was extracted by Julian C Walton and reprinted in *The Irish Ancestor* in 1978 [208]. The INA holds the original Tithe Valuations for Athboy, County Meath, from 1797 to 1801.

As a direct consequence of the French Revolutionary Wars at the end of the eighteenth century the British Parliament introduced a *Defence of the Realm Act* in 1798. This was designed to identify all men throughout the country between the ages of 15 and 60 who were not at that time involved in any military activities. The aim was to locate potential recruits for the *Posse Comitatus* (Home Guard) should the French be successful in landing on British soil. In every parish of each county parish constables were required to record the names and occupations of all able-bodied men in the stated age bracket and to specifically identify the millers, bakers and wagon and barge owners. Unfortunately very few of these lists survive for most counties, and where they do they are in a variety of locations. There is a complete set for Buckinghamshire in the Stowe Manuscripts Collection at the British Library, although the returns for the county (from a slightly different copy in the county archives) have been edited and usefully indexed [209] with an interesting background commentary by Dr Ian Beckett. Those few surviving for Northamptonshire are in the County Record Office in Northampton; for other counties JSWG has indicated [210] where these lists may be found.

It is likely that the 1798 Act caused the authorities at Stockton upon Tees in County Durham to conduct the census there in 1799 which was referred to by Brewster (see 1794); the Stockton listing was, therefore, not a true census but a *Posse Comitatus* list. As the original material is now lost and only Brewster's reference survives we shall never know for certain.

Following the 1798 rebellion in Ireland, the government offered compensation to individuals who had suffered losses. Lists of the claimants from the counties of Carlow, Down, Dublin, Galway, Kildare, Mayo, Sligo, Wexford and Wicklow are in the INA, so providing yet further census-type data. A list of rebel prisoners in Limerick gaol in 1798 was published in the *Journal of the North Munster Antiquarian Society* in 1966. Also surviving from 1798 is a Voters' List for Drogheda, County Louth, Ireland; this was published, with a similar listing for 1802, in the *County Louth Archaeological and Historical Society Journal* in 1984.

The Militia Pay Lists and Muster Rolls for 1799 and 1800 for County Antrim and County Down, Ireland are in PRONI. A 1799 listing of Protestant Householders in Templecrone, County Donegal, Ireland appeared in *The Irish Ancestor* in 1984.

In 1800, at Melbury Osmond in Dorset a local census was undertaken, very much on the same lines as the censuses which were conducted throughout the remainder of the nineteenth century; in fact this census has often erroneously been attributed to 1801, the style being so similar to subsequent surveys. The original returns are now in the Dorset Record Office. The census taken at Sandford, Devon during this year was referred to above (see 1775). Lists of Freeholders in County Longford, Ireland from 1800 to 1835 are in the Genealogical Office, Dublin.

Finally in 1800, as a result of the lobbying, the public debate, the pamphlets and the correspondence, another *Population Bill* was laid before Parliament; Abbot, to whom Rickman had written four years previously, introduced the Bill on 19 November 1800 and this time the attempt was a success, the Act coming into force during the following year. Thus a nation-wide census was held on 10 March 1801 and a similar national enumeration has taken place every ten years since then (except in 1941 when Britain was otherwise busy). Rickman was made responsible for organising the 1801 census which was taken through local parish officers - in fact the parish overseers - who remained responsible for the registration of electors, and a number of other duties associated with censuses, until *the Representation of the People Act* of 1918. Rickman, with the national figures available to him, which included information derived from parish registers prior to 1801, was able to compile various statistical analyses of the census results and then estimate the growth of the nation's population through the seventeenth and eighteenth centuries.

Even the regular, decennial censuses henceforth imposed on every community in the country did not diminish enthusiasm in some areas for conducting local surveys and enumerations and listings of inhabitants; on some occasions with details of names, ages, addresses, occupations and other details which were not requested on a national basis until much later in the nineteenth century.

For example, there was the September 1806 census of Jersey, ordered by the Lieutenant Governor, containing 4,363 names of heads of families and numbers of men, women, boys and girls; the original returns are in the Jersey Government Office but there are copies which have been indexed by the Channel Islands Family History Society in La Société Jersiaise Library and in their own library. Rev Joseph Dunn took a census of his Roman Catholic congregation in Preston, Lancashire in 1820, indicating names, ages, family relationships and addresses; the 8,500 entries were transcribed and published by Margaret Purcell in 1993. There was the 1817 survey by Rev Henry Comyn in Hampshire of the combined parishes Boldre and Brockenhurst into which he incorporated sketch maps of the locations of houses, exact dates of birth of many parishioners, schools which some children were attending and other intimate details; the original manuscript notes are held by Hampshire County Library Service, but an illustrated, indexed transcription by Jude F James was published in 1982 [211]. There was the 1825 census of Hungerford, Berkshire taken on 1 January that year; it names the heads of households and their children but not the names of their wives. As it was updated in 1826, 1833, 1834 and 1835 and separate revisions were prepared in 1828, 1829, 1830 and 1831, which are all in the county record office, Donald Steel [212] believes these censuses were connected with outdoor relief under the poor laws. There was the 1832 listing, now in the county archives, [213] of the inhabitants of Summertown, Oxford taken by the incumbent, but with some marvellous uninhibited biographical comments by J Badcock. There was the 1833 census of Southill, Bedfordshire, the returns now held in the county archives [214]. There was the 1834-36 analysis of Bowerchalke, Wiltshire, which gave not only names of the inhabitants but for each their date and place of birth, baptism and marriage. There was the 1837 census of Houghton Conquest in Bedfordshire, the original documents [215] of which are in that county's archives, and for September of the same year, the names of owners, occupiers and descriptions of property in Grandborough, Warwickshire, on lists in the county record office. [216]. The 1838 census of Marshchapel, Lincolnshire is in the Grimsby archives [217], among Dr John Parkinson's private papers.

In 1803 two *Defence Acts* were passed by Parliament in a further attempt (see the 1798 *Defence Act*) to anticipate civil defence procedures needed should the French invade Britain. *Levee en Masse* lists were required to be drawn up by the parish constables. The first Act, in June, sought the same details as the 1798 Act; but the second Act, in July 1803, required the equivalent of a complete census of the entire population by name, on a variety of schedules which requested numerous other personal details. Many of the schedules have not survived, or possibly were never completed, but the information required on the first schedule was the name, age, occupation, marital status, infirmity and number of children under ten years of age for each male between the ages of 17 and 55; on the second schedule the names of all householders, their ages and occupations, whether they were Quakers or aliens, and how many males and females there were in those households; on the third schedule the non-combatants who would require evacuating had to be listed by name, age and occupation - in practice this implied the women, children, old and infirm; the fourth schedule comprised men between 17 and 55 who would form the pioneers and special constables; the fifth schedule listed the purveyors and carriers of strategic supplies, such as millers, bakers, wagon and barge owners, guides, wagoners, stockmen and the numbers of stock and amounts of fodder that would have also to be moved in the event of an invasion. For some counties digests were made of these complex schedules; only summaries of the figures have survived for other counties, among the Lieutenancy papers and Privy Council records. Most of the original schedules were retained by those who completed them and so disappeared either into private collections or were destroyed. Some schedules are identified in Appendix II, if no 1801 civil census with names of individuals for that parish has been found.

What has been described as 'Don's Military Census' was conducted on Jersey in 1815 by parishes on the orders of Lieutenant General Don, the Commander in Chief and also the Lieutenant Governor of the Island. However, the document contains not only names, ages, and ranks in the militia but also names and (some) occupations of all men from 17 to 80 and the numbers of women, boys and girls. The names are listed alphabetically in each *vingtaine* of the twelve Jersey parishes. The original census is in the Jersey Government Office but there are copies in the libraries of La Société Jersiaise and the Channel Islands Family History Society.

The information required for the 1801, 1811 and subsequent decennial censuses prior to 1841 has already been mentioned at the beginning of this Cameo. But, as discussed before, for a variety of reasons additional details were collected and recorded for a number of parishes and registration districts. Some of these are identified in Appendix II. The author would welcome others being drawn to his attention.

In conclusion it should not be overlooked that whilst specific towns or parishes, for which lists of individuals' names were made, are identified in Appendix I, there were in addition many national surveys for taxation or religious or military purposes which contain names of people. Researchers are accordingly urged to refer to such surveys described in this Cameo at the locations indicated. The appropriate archivist will be able to advise on the availability of these pre-1841 censuses and population listings.

Appendix I - Censuses with individuals' names

The years for which there are listings for an entire county are given first, in chronological order, followed by listings in alphabetical order for specific areas of that county. The existence of a nineteenth century decennial census in a county is indicated last, **but by the year only**; the exact areas covered by these can be found in Appendix II. Attention is also drawn to over 100 national tax and other listings, identified in the Index, many of them containing names of individals, often compiled on a county basis; their whereabouts are identified on the relevant pages in the main text.

Aberdeenshire	1695; 1801, 1811.
Anglesey	1801, 1821.
Antrim	1740, 1776, 1799, 1800; 1821 (1820).
Armagh	1740, 1753, 1766, 1793; Drumcree 1737; 1821.
Ayrshire	1821, 1831.
Banffshire	1821
Bedfordshire	1297; Barton-le-Cley 1603 (1512, 1551, 1671); Cardington 1782; Hinwick 1778, 1788; Houghton Conquest 1712, 1837; Milton Ernest 1788; Pavenham 1699; Podington 1778, 1788; Renhold 1773; Southill 1833; Thurleigh 1788; 1811, 1821, 1831.
Berkshire	Hungerford 1825-1835; 1801, 1811, 1821, 1831.
Berwickshire	1811, 1831.
Buckinghamshire	1798; West Wycombe 1760; 1801, 1811, 1821, 1831.
Bute, Isle of	1821.
Caernarvonshire	1597.
Cambridgeshire	Cambridge 1749; Diocese of Ely 1716-44; 1801, 1811, 1821, 1831.
Cardiganshire	1821.
Carlow	1767.
Carmarthenshire	1821.
Cavan	1611-13; Kildallon 1703-04; 1801, 1821.
Cheshire	1723; Diocese of Chester 1705; 1801, 1811, 1821, 1831.
Clare	1745; 1821.
Cork	1700-52, 1757, 1766; Cork City 1783; Shadon 1793.
Cornwall	1334-1434; 1801, 1811, 1821.
Cumberland	Carlisle 1377, 1787, 1796; Diocese of Carlisle 1676; Maryport 1765; Whitehaven 1762; 1811, 1821.
Denbighshire	1811, 1821.
Derbyshire	1633; Melbourne 1695; 1801, 1811, 1821, 1831.
Devon	1334-1434, 1549; Coleridge 1670; Sandford 1775, 1783, 1790, 1793, 1800; Wembworthy 1779; 1801, 1811, 1821.
Donegal	1612-13; 1740; Cudolf 1782; Templecrome 1799.
Dorset	Beaminster 1775; Corfe Castle 1790; Lyme Regis 1695-1702. Melbury Osmond 1800; Poole 1574; Puddleton 1724-25; 1801, 1811, 1821, 1831.
Down	1740-77, 1789, 1799-1800; Downpatrick 1708.
Dublin	Castlemack 1793; Dublin City 1736, 1767, 1778-82; St Michan's Dublin 1711-1835; 1801, 1811, 1831.
Dumfriesshire	1801, 1811, 1821.

Durham.	1821.
Essex	Bocking 1793; Colchester 1377; Harlow 1797; 1801, 1811, 1821, 1831.
Fermanagh	1612-13, 1788, 1794-99, 1796-1802; 1821
Fifeshire	1821.
Flintshire	1811, 1821, 1831.
Forfarshire (Angus)	1801.
Galway	1727; Loughrea 1791; Galway Town 1794; 1821.
Gloucestershire	1608; Bristol 1695; Olveston 1742; Uley 1795; 1801, 1811, 1821, 1831.
Guernsey	1821.
Hampshire	Boldre & Brockenhurst 1817; 1801, 1811, 1821, 1831.
Herefordshire	1680; 1801, 1811, 1831.
Hertfordshire	1801, 1821.
Huntingdonshire	1549; Diocese of Ely 1716-44; 1811, 1821.
Inverness-shire	1801, 1831.
Isle of Man	Douglas 1730, 1757, 1784.
Jersey	1750, 1806, 1815; St Lawrence 1788.
Kent	1334-1434; Canterbury (and Diocese) 1565; Goodnestone 1676; Hayes 1790; New Romney 1695; Ramsgate 1773, 1785, 1796; Sandwich 1571; Wingham Petty Div 1705; Wrotham 1676; 1801, 1811, 1821, 1831.
Kerry	1821.
Kildare	1831.
Kilkenny	1785; Graiguenamanagh 1797; St John Kilkenny City 1715; Knocktopher 1797; 1821.
Kincardineshire	1811, 1821.
King's (Offaly)	1801 (1802), 1821.
Kirkcudbrightshire	1821, 1831.
Lanarkshire	1821.
Lancashire	1687; Lancaster 1784; Preston 1820; 1801, 1811, 1821, 1831.
Leicestershire	1801, 1811, 1821, 1831.
Leitrim	1791; Mohill 1792; 1821.
Limerick	1761, 1776; Limerick City 1793; 1821.
Lincolnshire	1676; Swinderby 1771, 1791; 1801, 1811, 1821, 1831.
London *	1377, 1638, 1640, 1677, 1695; Diocese of 1705, 1723- 48, 1765, 1766, 1780; 1801, 1811, 1821, 1831.
Londonderry (Derry)	1831.
Longford	1800-35; Shrule 1731.
Louth	1756, 1786-92; Drogheda 1798, 1802; Dromiskin 1791.
Mayo	Westport 1785-1815; 1821.
Meath	Athboy 1797; 1821.
Middlesex	Ealing 1599; 1801, 1811, 1821, 1831.
Midlothian	1801, 1811, 1821, 1831.
Monaghan	Carrickmacross 1777.
Montgomeryshire	1831.
Morayshire	1811.
Norfolk	Norwich 1570; 1801, 1811, 1821, 1831.
Northamptonshire	Aynho 1740; Cogenhoe 1618-1628; Courteenhall 1587; 1811, 1821, 1831.
Northumberland	1811, 1821, 1831.
Nottinghamshire	1549; Clayworth 1676, 1688; West Retford 1794; 1801, 1811, 1821, 1831.
Orkney Isles	1821.
Oxfordshire	1549; Cuxham 1772; Kidlington 1545; Oxford 1377; Summertown 1832; 1801, 1811, 1821, 1831.
Perthshire	St Madoes 1596; 1811, 1821, 1831.
Queen's (Laois)	1758-75; 1821.

* normally refers only to   the City of London, although Westminster may also be included.

Renfrewshire	1695; 1821.
Ross-shire	1821.
Roxburghshire	1831.
Shropshire	1801, 1811, 1821, 1831.
Somerset	Frome 1785; 1801, 1811, 1821, 1831
Staffordshire	Archdeaconry 1532; Biddulph 1779; Bradeley 1755, 1763, 1772; Stafford 1622; Stoke-upon-Trent 1701; 1801, 1811, 1821, 1831.
Suffolk	1676; Ipswich 1587; 1801, 1811, 1821, 1831.
Surrey	1801, 1811, 1821, 1831.
Sussex	1297, 1334-1434; Rye 1488; 1801, 1811, 1821, 1831.
Sutherlandshire	1811.
Tipperary	1766; 1776; 1821.
Tyrone	1740; 1821.
Warwickshire	Chilvers Coton 1684; Coventry 1523; Fenny Compton 1698; Grandborough 1837; Rugby 1792; Stratford-upon-Avon 1765; Warwick 1587; 1801, 1811, 1821, 1831.
Waterford	1766, 1792; Waterford City 1778; 1821.
Westmeath	1761-88; 1801 (1802).
Westmorland	1787; 1801, 1811.
Wexford	1776; Ballycanew 1792; Ferns 1789.
Wicklow	1745; Newcastle 1792-96.
Wigtownshire and Minnigaff	1684.
Wiltshire	Bowerchalke 1834-36; Box 1684; Cheverall, Little 1785; Chisleden 1787; Colerne 1774; Corsham 1770; Ditchridge 1684; Donhead 1695; Haslebury 1684; Marlborough 1600, 1601; Salisbury 1635; Stanton St Bernard 1744; Swindon 1673; 1801, 1811, 1821, 1831.
Worcestershire	Worcester St Andrew 1795; 1801, 1811, 1821, 1831.
Yorkshire	1549; Diocese of York 1735; Hornsea 1450; Hull 1377; Wakefield 1723; York 1272, 1559, 1680 [17]; 1801, 1811, 1821, 1831.

Appendix II - Decennial censuses: 1801 to 1831

To locate the custodian of these returns contact the archivist for the county or region concerned.   [* all persons named, often with ages]

1801

Aberdeenshire
Birse *
Peterhead

Anglesey
Amlwch

Berkshire
Binfield *
Brightwell *
Hampstead Marshall
Pangbourne
Tilehurst

Buckinghamshire
Beachampton
Iver
Wooburn

Cambridgeshire
Cambridge St Edward
Cambridge St Mary the Great
Ely St Mary
Girton
Hinxton * (1802)
Little Wilbraham

Cavan
Enniskin (part) (1802)

Cheshire
Marbury

Cornwall
St Hilary

Derbyshire
Clowne *
Eckington
Morley

Smalley
Stanton by Bridge

Devon
Barnstaple * (1803)
Bickleigh *
Exeter S Mary Steps * (1803)
Exeter St Paul * (1803)
Morthoe (possibly 1811)
Tawton, North * (1803)

Dorset
Corfe Castle (1803)
Dorchester (1800)
Melbury Osmond * (1800)
Oborne *
Poole (1803)
Sturminster Newton *
Winterbourne St Martin

Dublin
Castleknock * (Prots)
Clonsilla
  & Mulhuddart * (Prots)

Dumfriesshire
Annan *

Essex
Ashdon
Baddow, Little
Debden
Norton Mandeville
Rainham
Rochford (1803)
Terling
Toppesfield

Forfarshire (Angus)
Dundee

Gloucestershire
Badminton, Great
Bristol St Augustine the Less
Hawkesbury
Olveston *
Tortworth
Woolaston * (1800)

Hampshire
Calbourne * (1803)
Exton
Fordingbridge
Lymington

Herefordshire
Stoke Edith

Hertfordshire
Barkway & Reed *
Hitchin
Therfield (1803)

Inverness-shire
Lewiston

Kent
Borden
Bromley
Deal
Eastry
Folkestone
Malling, West
Smarden

King's (Offaly)
Ballyboggan (1802) (C of I)
Ballyboy (1802) (C of I)
Castlejordan (1802) (C of I)
Clonmacnoise (1802) (C of I)
Drumcullin (1802) (C of I)
Eglish (1802) (C of I)

Gallen (1802) (C of I)
Killoughey (1802) (C of I)
Lynally (1802) (C of I)
Rynagh (1802) (C of I)
Tullamore (1802) (C of I)

Lancashire

Croston
Edgeworth * (Turton)
Elton (Bury)
Liverpool
Whalley (part)
Winwick with Hulme *

Leicestershire

Bruntingthorpe
Houghton on the Hill
Thurcaston

Lincolnshire

Ponton, Little
Whaplode

London, City of

St Helen Bishopsgate
St Nicholas Acons
St Sepulchre

Meath

Agher (1802) (C of I)
Ardagh (1802) (C of I)
Castlerickard (1802) (C of I)
Castletown Kilpatrick (1802)
  (C of I)
Clonard (1802) (C of I)
Clongill (1802) (C of I) *
Drumconrath (1802) (Cof I) *
Duleek (1802) (C of I)
Emlagh (1802) (C of I)
Julianstown (1802) (C of I)
Kells (1802) (C of I)
Kentstown (1802) (C of I) *
Kilbeg (1802) (C of I)
Kilmainhamwood (1802)
  (C of I)
Kilskyre (1802) (C of I)
Knockmark (1802) (C of I)
Laracor (1802) (C of I)
Moynalty (1802) (C of I)
Navan (1802) (C of I)
Newtown (1802) (C of I)
Raddenstown (1802) (C of I)
Rathcore (1802) (C of I)
Rathkenny (1802) (C of I)

Rathmolyon (1802) (C of I)
Ratoath (1802) (C of I)
Roberstown (1802) (C of I)
Skyrne (1802) (C of I)
Slane (1802) (C of I)
Syddan (1802) (C of I)
Tara (1802) (C of I)
Trim (1802) (C of I)

Middlesex

Chelsea St Luke
Chiswick
Hampstead
Hendon
St James Piccadilly
St Margaret (few names)
St Mary le Strand

Midlothian

Stow *

Norfolk

Baconsthorpe
Beeston next Mileham
Hethersett
Illington *
Ingworth
Southrepps (1800)
Starston
Thorpe Episcopi nxt Norwich
Weston Longville
Winfarthing *
Woodton

Nottinghamshire

Eakring
Kinoulton (copy)
Norwell (1803)
Welbeck *

Oxfordshire

Cottisford
Stoke Lyne
Stonesfield

Shropshire

Felton, West
Longford

Somerset

Babcary
Huntspill
Monkton Combe (1803)

Radstock (1803)
Wincanton

Staffordshire

Biddulph
Lichfield St Michael
Stafford St Mary
Walsall
Wednesbury

Suffolk

Brome
Holton St Mary
Horringer
Ipswich St Clement
Ipswich St Peter
Walsham le Willows
Worlingworth

Surrey

Bletchingley
Chobham *
Clapham
Ewhurst
Guildford
Mortlake
Newdigate
Nutfield
Oxted

Sussex

Hurstpierpoint (1803)
Kirdford * (1803)
Ticehurst

Warwickshire

Brinklow
Church Lawford
Hillmorton

Westmeath

Ballyloughloe (1802) (C of I)
Castletown Delvin (1802)
  (C of I)
Clonarney (1802) (C of I)
Drumraney (1802) (C of I)
Enniscoffey (1802) (C of I)
Kilbridepass (1802) (C of I)
Kilcleagh (1802) (C of I)
Killalon (1802) (C of I)
Killough (1802) (C of I)
Killua (1802) (C of I)
Killucan (1802) (C of I)
Leney (1802) (C of I)

Moyliscar (1802) (C of I)
Rathconnell (1802) (C of I)

Westmorland

Beetham

Wiltshire

Box *
Highworth
Horningsham
Keevil (part)
Steeple Ashton (1800)

Worcestershire

Kidderminster (part)

Yorkshire

Bracewell
Elland-cum-Greetland
Hedon
Hipperholme-cum-Brighouse
Langfield
Leeds (township - part)
Lissett

Midgley
Newton Kyme
Sandal Magna
Spofforth
Swinton
Thrybergh
Tong
Westow
York St Giles

1811

Aberdeenshire

Birse * (1812)
Glencanar * (1812)

Bedfordshire

Kensworth

Berkshire

Blewbury
Brightwell
Cumnor
Newnham

Berwickshire

Ladykirk

Buckinghamshire

Lathbury (draft only)
Ravenstone

Cambridgeshire

Balsham
Cambridge St Edward
Cambridge St Mary the Great
Ely St Mary
Hildersham (1810)
Trumpington

Cheshire

Alderley *

Cornwall

Poundstock

Cumberland

Isel

Denbighshire

Clocaenog

Derbyshire

Crich
Findern *
Hope
Littleover *
Mickleover *
Morley
Stanton by Bridge

Devon

Doddiscombsleigh *
Morthoe (possibly 1801)

Dorset

Corfe Castle *
Whitchurch Canonicorum
(part)

Dumfriesshire

Annan *

Essex

Ardleigh
Ashdon (1810)
Bradwell juxta Mare
Brightlingsea
Clacton, Great
Colchester St Leonard
Elmstead
Gestingthorpe
Hatfield Broad Oak
Horndon on the Hill
Leyton
Middleton

Mundon
Parndon, Great
Rainham
Rochford
Saffron Walden
Saint Lawrence
Sandon
Terling
Thorrington
Tilbury juxta Clare
Toppesfield
Wakes Colne (1809)
Walthamstow
Wickford
Witham
Woodham Walter

Flintshire

Mold

Gloucestershire

Badminton, Great
Bristol St Augustine the Less
Horsley
Mickleton
Naunton
Rendcombe
Tortworth

Hampshire

Calbourne
Fawley
Fordingbridge
Kings Worthy
Lymington
Rotherwick

Herefordshire

Lucton

Huntingdonshire
Alwalton

Kent
Borden
Canterbury (part)
Deal
Goudhurst
Hardres, Lower
Luddesdown (1810)
Maidstone (part)
Smarden

Kincardineshire
Dunnottar

Lancashire
Ashton under Lyne
Bolton, Great
Croston
Whalley
Wigan (part)

Leicestershire
Bruntingthorpe
Loughborough (part)
Market Harborough
Thurcaston

Lincolnshire
Fleet
Waddington
Whaplode
Winteringham (part)

London, City of
Allhallows Lombard Street
St Ann Blackfriars (part)
St Benet Paul's Wharf
St Benet Sherhog
St Botolph Bishopsgate
St John Bap upon Walbrook
St Mary Woolchurch Haw
St Mary Woolnoth
St Nicholas Acons
St Peter Cornhill
St Peter Paul's Wharf
St Sepulchre Holborn
St Swithin London Stone
St Thomas Apostle

Middlesex
Brentford, New (1810)

Hackney St John
Hampstead
Hendon
St Margaret (some names)
St Mary le Strand

Midlothian
Dalkeith

Morayshire
Dallas *

Norfolk
Baconsthorpe
Bircham, Great
Buckenham, Old
Tuddenham, East (1810)
Wacton Magna
Winfarthing *

Northamptonshire
Ashby, Cold
Billing, Great
Evenley
Walgrave

Northumberland
Newcastle All Saints (part)

Nottinghamshire
Gotham
Kinoulton
Laxton
Newark
Radford (1813)
Retford, West
Worksop

Oxfordshire
Bletchingdon
Drayton (1813) (part)
Rotherfield Greys
Stonesfield
Yarnton

Perthshire
Longforgan with
    Invergowrie

Shropshire
Longnor (1812)

Somerset
Ashcott
Brockley
Cadbury, North
Camerton
Chilton Polden
Coker, East
Littleton, High
Selworthy
Stowey
Wincanton

Staffordshire
Colwich
Newcastle under Lyme
Walsall (part)
Wednesbury

Suffolk
Clare (1809)
Glemsford
Ipswich St Clement
Ipswich St Peter
Metfield
Swilland
Wickhambrook

Surrey
Bletchingley
Chobham
Clapham
Croydon
Mitcham
Mortlake
Newington
Oxted
Southwark St Saviour
Stoke d'Albernon

Sussex
Grinstead, East
Hurstpierpoint
Kirdford
Lewes St Michael
Rusper
Ticehurst

Sutherland
Assynt, Farr & Golspie
Reay

Warwickshire
Barston *
Coleshill

Cubbington
Warwick St Mary

Westmorland

Beetham
Crosby Ravensworth

Wiltshire

Foxley
Grittleton
Malmesbury (part)
Manningford Abbots (1810)
Woodborough

Worcestershire

Bromsgrove
Kidderminster (part)

Yorkshire

Allerston
Beeford
Boynton
Calverley
Carleton in Craven
Dunnington
Elland-cum-Greetland
Farsley
Hilston
Hipperholme-cum-Brighouse
Honley
Kilburn
Lissett
Marfleet
Middleton upon Leven
Midgley

Otterington, South
Patrington
Skipwith (part)
Snaith
Sowerby
Tankersley * (1809)
Thirsk
Todmorden & Walsden
Tong
Welton
Yeadon
York St Cuthbert
York St Giles
York St Martin
York St Maurice

1821

Anglesey

Beaumaris

Antrim

Lisburn (1820)

Armagh

Derryhale *
Kilmore *

Ayrshire

St Quivox
Stevenston * (1820)

Banffshire

Dufftown * (1820)
Mortlach *

Bedfordshire

Bedford St Peter
Blunham
Haynes

Berkshire

Brightwalton (part)
Brimpton * (1822)
Caversham
Earley (Sonning)
East Hendred
Hungerford *

Buckinghamshire

Chesham (part)
Chenies (draft)
Iver
Olney
Princes Risborough

Bute, Isle of

Rothesay * (1820)

Cambridgeshire

Cambridge St Benedict
Cambridge St Edward
Downham
Duxford

Cardiganshire

Llandygwydd

Carmarthenshire

Llanarthney

Cavan

Annageliffe *
Ballymachugh *
Castlerahan *
Castleterra *
Crosserlough *
Denn *
Drumlumman *
Drung *

Kilbride *
Kilmore *
Kinawley *
Larah *
Lurgan *
Mullagh *
Munteronnaught *

Cheshire

Alderley *
Rostherne *

Clare

Ennis (part)

Cornwall

Bodmin
Boyton *
Veryan *

Cumberland

Holme Cultram
Newton Reigny (part)
Skelton (part)

Denbighshire

Gresford (part)
Henllan

Derbyshire

Chesterfield (part)
Crich (part)

Doveridge
Eckington
Mackworth *
Mickleover
Normanton, South
Ockbrook
Stanton by Bridge
Ticknall (part)

Devon

Axminster
Bickleigh
Clyst St George *
Dean Prior
Exeter Holy Trinity
Fremington
Rewe

Dorset

Broadwinsor
Compton Abbas
Corfe Castle *
Horton *
Litton Cheney
Marnhull
Shaftesbury St James
Thornford *
Wimborne St Giles (1822)
Winterborne Whitechurch
Woodlands *

Dumfriesshire

Annan *

Durham

Durham St Oswald (part)

Essex

Ardleigh
Baddow, Little
Beaumont cum Moze
Braintree *
Colchester St Leonard
Debden
Finchingfield
Horndon on the Hill
Leyton
Mistley
Tilbury juxta Clare
Tolleshunt Major
Walthamstow
Wanstead
Woodham Walter
Writtle

Fermanagh

Aghalurcher * (part)
Derryvullen *

Fifeshire

Abdie

Flintshire

Northop

Galway

Aran
Athenry
Kilcomeen
Kilconickny
Killimoredaly
Kilreekill
Kiltullagh
Loughrea (part)

Gloucestershire

Aust
Badminton, Great
Barnsley *
Bisley
Bristol St Augustine the Less
Mickleton
Stratton
Stroud
Woolaston

Guernsey

The Vale *

Hampshire

Fawley
Fordingbridge
Headley
Newchurch (part) (copy)
Ryde
Tisted, East *
Wherwell
Winchester St Bartholomew *
Winchester S John (pt)(1820)
Winchester St Peter (part)
Winnall (1820)

Hertfordshire

Digswell *
Hitchin (part)

Huntingdonshire

Alwalton
Bluntisham
Godmanchester

Kent

Beckenham
Deal
Penshurst
Rochester St Nicholas
Thanington

Kerry

Kilcummin

Killkenny

Aglish *
Clonmore
Fiddown
Kilmacow
Poleroan
Portnascully
Rathkyran
Whitechurch

Kincardineshire

Dunnottar

King's (Offaly)

Aghacon *
Birr *
Ettagh *
Kilcolman *
Kinnitty *
Letterluna *
Roscomroe *
Rocrea *
Seirkieran *

Kirkcudbrightshire

Kirkcudbright * (1819)
Lochrutton

Lanarkshire

Lesmahagow

Lancashire

Bolton, Great
Broughton
Eccleston (part)
Penketh (Prescot)

Leicestershire

Allexton
Kilworth, South
Lutterworth
Melton Mowbray
Quorndon

Leitrim

Carrigallen *

Limerick

Kilfinane

Lincolnshire

Barnetby le Wold
Canwick
Fleet
Lincoln St Martin
Waddington
Walcot by Folkingham

London, City of

Allhallows Lombard Str
St Benet Paul's Wharf
St Benet Sherehog
St Helen Bishopsgate
St Katherine Coleman
St Margaret Lothbury
St Mary Abchurch
St Mary Woolchurch Haw
St Mary Woolnoth
St Nicholas Acons
St Peter Cornhill
St Sepulchre Holborn
St Swithin London Stone
St Thomas Apostle

Mayo

Killalla (1820) (Prots)

Meath

Ardbraccan *
Ardsallagh *
Balrathboyne *
Bective *
Churchtown *
Clonmacduff *
Donaghmore *
Donaghpatrick *
Kilcooly *
Liscartan *
Martry *
Moymet *

Navan *
Newtownclonbun *
Rataine *
Rathkenny *
Trim *
Trimblestown *
Tullaghanogue *

Middlesex

Hackney St John
Hammersmith
Hendon
Marylebone St Marylebone
Poplar All Saints
St Mary le Strand
Westminster St Margaret
Willesden

Midlothian

Dalkeith
Glencorse

Norfolk

Baconsthorpe
Bodham
Bradfield
Buckenham, Old
Diss
Dunston
Haddiscoe
Harling, West
Sparham *
Tuttington
Winfarthing *
Wormegay

Northamptonshire

Badby * (1822)
Braunston
Draughton
Eye
Mears Ashby
Staverton
Woodford by Thrapston

Northumberland

Newcastle All SS (part)

Nottinghamshire

Gamston
Hawton
Kinoulton
Laxton
Radford

Syerston
Thorpe next Newark

Orkney Isles

Deerness *
Orphir *
St Andrews *
Sandwick *
South Ronaldsay & Burray *
Stromness *

Oxfordshire

Begbroke (part)
Bletchingdon
Britwell Salome
Caversham
Kiddington
Newington, North (1820)
Stonesfield
Woolvercot

Perthshire

Longforgan
Moulin *

Queen's (Laois)

Mountrath

Renfrewshire

Lochwinnoch

Ross & Cromarty

Barras (1819)
Uig (1819)

Shropshire

Ellesmere
Leighton
Longnor *
Shrewsbury Holy Cross
Shrewsbury St Chad
Shrewsbury St Mary
Wellington *

Somerset

Gasper *
Goathurst
Montacute
Stowey
Tintinhull
Wedmore
Wrington

Staffordshire

Tettenhall (1820)
Walsall (part)
Wednesbury

Suffolk

Aldham
Glemsford
Ipswich St Clement
Lowestoft
Pettistree
Playford
Southwold
Troston
Westley *
Wetherden
Wickhambrook

Surrey

Clapham
Mortlake
Oxted
Southwark Christchurch (pt)
Thursley

Sussex

Chiddingly *
Greatham
Grinstead, East (part)
Hailsham
Hartfield
Hastings St Mary (part)
Hoathly, East *
Hurstpierpoint
Rusper * (1822)

Tangmere *
Ticehurst (part)

Tipperary

Clonmel
Killinaffe * (part)
Modreeny (part)

Tyrone

Aghaloo (part)

Warwickshire

Austrey
Barston
Bedworth
Coleshill
Cubbington
Farnborough
Kineton
Rugby
Sheldon
Southam (copy)
Stivichall *
Tanworth in Arden *
Warwick St Mary

Waterford

Ballygunner * (part)
Waterford City * (part)

Wiltshire

Malmesbury (part)
Steeple Ashton
Stourton *

Stratford sub Castle
Sutton Veny
Trowbridge

Worcestershire

Bewdley
Bromsgrove
Himbleton
Kidderminster (part)
Ripple
Worcester St John

Yorkshire

Beeford
Boynton
Dunnington
Hedon
Heslerton, West
Hilston
Huntington
Marfleet
Ossett-cum-Gawthorpe *
Oswaldkirk
Sandal Magna
Spofforth
Stansfield
Swinton
Thirsk
Thornhill
Thurstonland
Tong
Warley
Yarm
Yeadon
York St Giles

1831

Ayrshire

Kirkeswald

Bedfordshire

Ampthill
Bedford St Mary
Ravensden
Silsoe

Berkshire

East Hendred
Hungerford *
Shellingford

Berwickshire

Ladykirk

Buckinghamshire

Nettleden *
Princes Risborough
Stoke Poges *

Cambridgeshire

Melbourn (copy)

Cheshire

Alderley *
Stockport (part)
Tattenhall (part)
Warburton *

Derbyshire

Smisby * (1830)
Whittington *

Devon

Coombe Martin *
Sidbury * (1829)

Dorset

Allington
Corfe Castle *
Langton Herring * (1830)
Ryme Intrinseca

Dublin

Dublin St Bride

Essex

Ashdon
Baddow, Little
Bentley, Little
Brightlingsea
Finchingfield *
Ingatestone *
Kelvedon (1830) (copy)
Leighs, Great (1829)
Leyton
Mundon
Steeple Bumpstead *
Tilbury juxta Clare *
Tolleshunt Major (part)
Upminster
Walthamstow
Woodham Walter
Wormingford

Flintshire

Mold (part)
Northop

Gloucestershire

Arlingham (1830)
Bisley
Bitton

Hampshire

Baughurst
Fawley
Fordingbridge

Herefordshire

Mordiford

Inverness-shire

Rothiemurchus

Kent

Dymchurch (1830)
Horsmonden
Ringwould
Sellindge

Shadoxhurst
Tenterden
Westwell (1830)

Kildare

Kilcullen (Protestants)

Kirkcudbrightshire

Lochrutton

Lancashire

Bolton, Great
Penketh (Prescot)
Whalley (part)

Leicestershire

Osgathorpe (part)

Lincolnshire

Canwick
Fillingham
Fleet
Gedney Hill
Grantham

London, City of

St Benet Paul's Wharf *
St Christopher-le-Stocks
St Clement Eastcheap
St Katherine Cree
St Margaret Lothbury
St Mary Abchurch
St Mary Woolchurch Haw
St Mary Woolnoth
St Matthew Friday Street
St Nicholas Acons
St Peter Cornhill
St Peter Paul's Wharf
St Peter Westcheap
St Thomas Apostle

Londonderry (Derry)

almost entire county

Middlesex

Hackney St John
Hammersmith
Harrow
Marylebone St Marylebone
Poplar All Saints
Stanmore, Little
Willesden (part)

Midlothian

Inveresk
Roslin (1830)

Montgomeryshire

Penstrowed

Norfolk

Alderford *
Coston *
Norwich S John de Sepulchre
Norwich St Peter Southgate

Northamptonshire

Badby *
Evenley *
Newnham *
Werrington (part)

Northumberland

Heddon on the Wall * (1830)

Nottinghamshire

Beckingham
Blyth
Mansfield
Walkeringham

Oxfordshire

Bletchingdon
Oxford St Giles * (1832) (pt)
Stonesfield *

Perthshire

Longforgan

Roxburghshire

Jedburgh
Kelso (1830)
Melrose

Shropshire

Bishops Castle (part)
Ellesmere
Shrewsbury St Julian

Somerset

Brislington
Stone Easton *
Stowey (1829)
Wedmore

Staffordshire

Blymhill
Lichfield St Mary
Sedgley
Walsall (part)

Suffolk

Athelington
Brome
Cretingham
Ipswich St Margaret
Ipswich St Peter
Lowestoft
Westley *
Wickhambrook

Surrey

Chobham
Newington St Mary
Southwark Christchurch
Southwark St Saviour
Streatham

Sussex

Dean, East *
Grinstead, East (part)
Hailsham
Hastings St Clement
Hastings St Mary
Lewes St John
Rusper * (1829)
Uckfield

Warwickshire

Arrow (part)
Astley
Bidford
Bulkington
Coleshill
Halford
Kingsbury
Stratford, Old
Stratford-upon-Avon
Warwick St Mary
Warwick St Nicholas

Wiltshire

Bromham
Downton
Malmesbury (part)
Stockton (part)
Stourton
Sutton Veny

Worcestershire

Belbroughton
Kidderminster (part)
Tardebigge
Wolverley *

Yorkshire

Boynton
Hallam, Nether
Hedon
Hipperholme-cum-Brighouse
Snaith
Spofforth
Swinton
Warmsworth * (1829)
Yeadon

Notes & references

1. Numbers I. vv 1-54.

2. a villein had an interest in 60 acres and owned 4 oxen. A bordar had an interest in 15-30 acres and owned 2 oxen. A serf had an interest in 5 acres and owned 1 ox. A ploughland was the area which a ploughteam (8 oxen) could plough in an agricultural year; this amounted to approximately 120 acres but obviously depended on the terrain.

3. e.g. Hilary Jenkinson, Mrs (formerly V Rickards, Miss). *An Early Bedfordshire Taxation (1237)*. Bedfordshire Historical Record Society. Vol 2. (1914) p 225.

4. F Collins (ed). *Register of the Freemen of the City of York. Vol I. 1272-1558*. Surtees Soc. Vol 96. (1896).

5. in 1290, 1294, 1295, 1296, 1297, 1301, 1306, 1307, 1309, 1313, 1315, 1319, 1322, 1327, 1332; see also: Bedfordshire Historical Record Society. Vol 39 (1959) for a typical 1297 account and also: M W Beresford. Amateur Historian. Vol 3 No 8. (1958) pp 325-328.

6. ref: E 179 series; see also: M W Beresford. Amateur Historian. Vol 4 No 3. (1959) pp 101-109.

7. in East Sussex Record Office.

8. in Coventry City Record Office; see also: VCH Warwickshire Vol 8 p 4.

9. ref: E 36 and E 315 series.

10. J R Western. *The English Militia in the Eighteenth Century, 1660-1802*. (1965);and Lindsay Boynton. *The Elizabethan Militia 1558-1638*. (1967).

11. in Amateur Historian. Vol 4 No 3. (1959) p 104.

12. Ann J Kettle (ed). *A List of Families in the Archdeaconry of Stafford 1532-3*. Staffordshire Record Society. 4th series. Vol 8. (1976).

13. in Vol 8. Part IV. (May 1937) pp 359-363.

14. ref: E 179/99/315 (Dev); E 179/122/143, 144, 146 (Hun); E 179/159/78, 182, 185 (Ntt); E 179/162/275 (Oxf); E179/203/251 (Ery); E 179/213/209 (Nry); E 179/208/211 (Wry); see also: M W Beresford. *The Poll Tax and Census of Sheep 1549*. Agr Hist Rev. Vol i. (1953) pp 9-15; and Vol ii (1954) pp 15-29.

15. Sue J Wright. *Easter Books*. Urban History Yearbook. (1985) pp 30-45; also LPS No.42 (Spring 1989) pp 18-31 & No.43 (Autumn 1989) pp 13-27.

16. J F Pound (ed). Norfolk Record Society. Vol 40. (1971) p 28.

17. F Collins (ed). *Register of the Freemen of the City of York. Vol II. 1559-1759*. Surtees Soc. Vol 102. (1899). John Malden's indexed *Register of York Freemen 1680 to 1986* was published in 1989 by Wm Sessions Ltd, York.

18. ref: Harl MS. 594-5.

19. Kent Record Office; the Canterbury parishes are ref: E/Q/1 (only parts of St. Martin and St. Paul survive); the Diocesan Communicants' Lists are ref: PRC 43/13/12.

20. Calendar State Papers. Vol 78. 29 Domestic. Elizabeth 1547-80. p 414

21. in E 377/1, 2, 3 & 4 and SP 12/142/33, 12/183/15, 12/200/61 etc; see also: D J Steel. *Sources for Roman Catholic and Jewish Genealogy and Family History*. NIPR. (1974).

22. for example: Roll No 1 1592-3 in Cath Rec Soc. Vol 18. (1916); Roll No 2 1593-4 in Cath Rec Soc. Vol 57. (1965); Roll No 3 1594-5 in Cath Rec Soc. Vol 61. (1970); Roll No 4 1595-6 with Roll No 3.

23. ref: 86 P/6.

24. ref: E 179 220/150.

25. Bulletin of the Board of Celtic Studies. Vol 8. Pt IV. (May 1937) pp 336-343.

26. in E 163/24/35; see also: K J Allison. *An Elizabethan Village Census*. Ealing LHS. Members Papers. No 2. (Oct 1962); and also: Bulletin of the Inst of Hist Research. Vol 36. No 93. (May 1963) pp 91-103.

27. ref: Harl MS. Vol 280. ff 157-172.

28. e.g. C W Forster *The State of the Church in the reigns of Elizabeth and James I as illustrated by documents relating to the Diocese of Lincoln. Vol I*. Lincolnshire Rec Soc. Vol 23. (1926) pp 253-353.

29. A J & R H Tawney. Economic History Review. Vol V. No 1. (Oct 1934) pp 25-64.

30. Historical Manuscripts Commission. 4th Report. (1947).

31. G H Dury. *The Population of Guernsey: An Essay in Historical Geography*. Geog. Vol 33. (1948) pp 61-69; see also: C A Robin. *Notes on the Population of Guernsey*. (1947).

32. ref: 71P/1.

33. ref: WS.L.D. 1721/1/4.

34. S O Addy. Derbyshire Arch & Nat Hist Soc. Vol VI. (Jan 1884) pp 49-74.

35. S Pender (ed). *Census of Ireland 1659*. Clearfield, Geneal Publ Co. Baltimore (1997).

36. Fifth Report of the Royal Commission on Historical Manuscripts, Pt I. Report & Appendix. (1876) pp 3 and 120-134; see also: Wilts Notes and Queries. Vol 7. (1911-13) pp 16-21, 79-84, 105-110, 162-167, 203-208, 260-265, 309-313, 343-347, 418-421, 450-452, 496-499; and also: J S W Gibson *Protestation Returns 1641-2*. FFHS. 1995.

37. J S W Gibson. *The Hearth Tax and Later Stuart Tax Lists and the Association Oath Rolls*. FFHS. (2nd edn 1996).

38. ref: H/2.

39. ref: MS 639 and VPIC/9.

40. ref: MS.Salt 33. [formerly catalogued as No 2112].

41. T Richards. *The Religious Census of 1676; An Inquiry into its Historical Value, Mainly in Reference to Wales*. Trans of the Honorable Socty of Cymmrodorion. (1927) Supp pp 1-118; [pp 1-15 are generic].

42. E A Whiteman. *The Compton Census of 1676: a critical edition*. Rec Soc & Econ Hist. New Series. Vol 10 (1986).

43. Kent Records. Vol 17. (1960) pp 153-174;

44. Mary J Dobson. *Original Compton Census Returns: The Shoreham Deanery*. Archaeologia Cantiana. Vol 94. (1978) pp 61-73.

45. in Transactions of the Cumberland and Westmoreland Antiquarian and Archaeological Society. Vol 51. New Series. (1952). Article 13 pp 137-141.

46. A S Langley. *A Religious Census of 1676 AD*. Lincolnshire Notes & Queries. Vol 16. No 2. (April 1920) pp 33-51.

47. E L Guilford. *Nottinghamshire in 1676*. Trans Thoroton Soc. Vol 28. (1924) pp 106-113; [transcribed from the Tanner MSS. (150 ff 28 and 129) in the Bodleian Library, Oxford].

48. D P Dymond. *Suffolk and the Compton Census of 1676*. Suffolk Review. Vol 3. (1966) pp 103-118.

49. (Rev D Bond). *The Compton Census - Peterborough*. Local Population Studies. Vol X. (1973) pp 71-74; but only six parish enumerations have been transcribed for this brief article.

50. P Laslett and J Harrison. *Clayworth and Cogenhoe*; in Historical Essays Presented to David Ogg. ed H E Bell and R L Ollard. (1963) pp 157-184; see also: P Laslett. *The World We Have Lost.* (1965).

51. H Gill and E L Guilford (eds). *The Rector's Book of Clayworth, Nottinghamshire.* (1910) pp 84-87.

52. C W F Goss. *The London Directories, 1677-1855.* (1932).

53. Jane E Norton. *Guide to the National and Provincial Directories of England and Wales, excluding London, published before 1856.* (1950). 2nd edn 1984.

54. Edward Evans. *Historical and Bibliographical Account of Almanacks, Directories etc in Ireland from the Sixteenth Century.* Dublin. (1897).

55. Main Papers 3 Dec 1680 No 321; as identified in Hist Man Com Vol XI. pt ii. (1887) pp 222-237.

56. W Scott (ed). *Parish Lists of Wigtownshire and Minnigaff.* Scottish Record Society. Vol 50. (1916).

57. Dr Richard Price. *Observations on Reversionary Payments on Schemes for Providing Annuities for Widows, and for Persons in Old Age; on the Method of Calculating the Values of Assurance on Lives; and on the National Debt.* (6th ed 1806). ed William Morgan. Vol 2. p 27 (footnote). This edition contains a number of typographical errors which were not present in the tables when they first appeared in his *Essay on the Population of England from the Revolution to the Present Time* in 1780. The 1st edn of *Observations* was published in 1771; as Price died in 1791 the last edition to which he personally made additions or corrections was the 5th, published in 1792. There was a 7th edn in 1812 to which population scholars often allude but the references in this Cameo are taken from my own copy of Price's *Observations*. Volume 1 of his *Observations* deals mostly with life expectancy data whereas volume 2 discusses population figures. All the references in this Cameo are taken from volume 2.

58. Colin R Chapman. *Marriage Laws, Rites, Records & Customs.* Lochin Publishing. (1997).

59. *London Inhabitants Within the Walls, 1695.* London Rec Soc (1996); see also E Jones & A V Judges. *London Population in the late 17th Century.* Econ Hist Rev. Vol VI. No 1. (Oct 1935) pp 45-63; and also: E Ralph & M E Williams (eds). *The Inhabitants of Bristol in 1696.* Bristol Record Society. (1968).

60. P H Styles. *A census of a Warwickshire Village in 1698.* Univ of Birm Hist Jour. Vol 3. No 1. (1951) pp 33-51; and, in general: E A Wrigley. *An Introduction to English Historical Demography.*(1966).

61. R E Chester Waters. *A Statutory List of the Inhabitants of Melbourne, Derbyshire in 1695.* Journal of the Derbyshire Arch & Natural History Society. Vol 7. (June 1885) pp 4-30.

62. W Gandy. *Association Oath Rolls of Lancashire.* (1921).

63. C R Webb. *The Association Oath Rolls of 1695.* Genealogists' Magazine. Vol 21. No 4. (Dec 1983) pp 120-123; see also : original rolls at PRO, in Class C 213.

64. e.g. D V Glass and D E C Eversley. *Population in History.* (1965).

65. K Walton. *The Distribution of Population in Aberdeenshire.* Scottish Geographical Magazine. Vol 66. No 1. (June 1950) pp 17-26.

66. The full title is: *Philosophical Transactions, giving some account of the Present Undertakings, Studies and Labours, of the ingenious in many considerable parts of the world.* It comprised papers often written by one party and then "communicated" via a second party to the Royal Society and subsequently read at meetings of its members prior to publication. A volume issued for one particular year was often not published until the subsequent year and hence some modern authors quote different dates for the same reference. In this Cameo the year for which, and not in which, the volume was issued is quoted and hereafter the publication is abbreviated to *Philosophical Transactions* or, in these notes, to Phil Trans Roy Soc. see: Phil Trans Roy Soc. Vol 22. (1700) pp 520-524; see also: Price. Op cit. p 23 (footnote) for Dublin; p 176 (footnote) for Maidstone.

67. J S W Gibson, M Medlycott and D Mills. *Land & Window Tax Assessments.* FFHS. 2nd ed. (1996).

68. Bedfordshire Historical Record Society. Vol 72 (1993) pp 3-23.

69. ref: M.4693.

70. see: R Talbot. *Fenton*. Stoke on Trent. (1977) pp 22-28.

71. The Irish Ancestor. Vol VIII No 2. (1976) pp 86-7.

72. J Collinson. *History and antiquities of the County of Somerset, collected from records made by Edmund Rack*. (1791). Vol 2 p 27.

73. Main Papers 1 Mar 1706 No 2249b. Calendared in Manuscripts of the House of Lords. Vol 6. (New Series). (1704-1706) pp 417-421.

74. see also: G Huelin. *Some 18th Century Roman Catholic Recusants*. Journal of Ecclesiastical History Vol VII. No 1. (April 1956) pp 61-68; and also: P Coverdale. *Essex Papists in 1706*. Essex Recusant. No 2. Vol 1. (1960) pp 16-29.

75. Main Papers 1 Mar 1706 No 2249c. Calendared in Manuscripts of the House of Lords. Vol 6. (New Series). (1704-1706) pp 421-423.

76. Yorkshire Archaeol Soc (Record Series) Vols 71, 72, 75 & 77 include the Visitation Returns for 1743.

77. e.g. in Wiltshire Record Office, Trowbridge; formerly in the Diocesan Archives at Salisbury, ref: 'Returns of Papists'; see also: Recusant History. Vol 7. No 1. (Jan 1963).

78. e.g. for York Diocese (but from Visitn. Returns) in Catholic Record Society. Vol 32. (1932) p 350.

79. ref: MS. 9550.

80. L Munby. *Hertfordshire Population Statistics, 1563-1801*. (1964).

81. Original at West Yorkshire Archive Service, Newstead Rd, Wakefield, WF1 2DE.

82. Bowtell's draft for *A History of Cambridge*. Vol 3 p 355; and C H Cooper. *Annals of Cambridge*. (1852). Vol 4.

83. Manx Soc. Vol 30. 3rd article. (1880).

84. Catholic Record Society. Vol 32. (1932) p 204; see also: Catholic Record Society. Vol 4. (1907) pp 368-373; and also: Northern Genealogist. Vol III. (1900) pp 84-88.

85. J Hunter. *Hallamshire*. (1819) p 21; the full title is *The History and Topography of the Parish of Sheffield in the County of York with Historical and descriptive Notices of the parishes of Ecclesfield, Hamsworth, Treeton and Whiston, and the Chapelry of Bradfield*; there were 'New and Enlarged' editions in 1869 and 1882 by Rev Alfred Gatty, vicar of Ecclesfield and Sub-dean of York.

86. Rare Book Dept Add. 2766 (15).7500.2.1./25; [St Helier and St Ouen are missing].

87. Phil Trans Roy Soc. Vol 48. (1754) pp 788-800; Vol 49. (1756) pp 877-890; Vol 50. (1757) pp 465-479; see also: W Maitland. *History of London...* . (1739) pp 533-542; [later editions were in 1756, 1772 and 1775]; and also: R Price. Op cit. pp 20, 21, 24 (footnotes) and 141.

88. P Morant. *History and antiquities of the County of Essex...* . (1768). Vol 2 p 1.

89. W Maitland. *History of Edinburgh from its foundation to the present time....Together with the ancient and present state of the town of Leith, etc.* . 1753. p 171.

90. R Price. Op cit. pp 57, 72 and 107.

91. ref: MS. Top. Glouc. c 4-5.

92. T D Fosbroke. *An Original History of the City of Gloucester....including also the original papers of....R Bigland*. (1819) p193.

93. Vols 71, 72, 75, 77.

94. R Price. Op cit. pp 70, 94, 95, 101 and 113.

95. in *Parliamentary Papers - Reports for Commissioners - Registrar General*. (Session 1847-8). Vol 25 pp 289-325.

96. Gentleman's Magazine. Vol 17. (1747) p 326.

97. W Maitland. Op cit. pp 217-218.

98. R Price. Op cit. p 57.

99. E Carter. *The History of the County of Cambridge from the earliest account to the Present Time.* (1753). pp 14-45.

100. ref: P25/28/1-2.

101. ref: Gough, Cambs, 76.

102. ref: CO 217. Vol 9 pp 226-227.

103. Channel Islands Family History Journal. No 38. (Spring 1988) pp 180-184.

104. R Price. Op cit. pp 34, 35, 70, 100, 101, 106 and 397; see also: Phil Trans Roy Soc. Vol 52. (1761) pp 140-141; Vol 61. (1771) pp 57-58; Vol 72. (1782) pp 53-57.

105. Phil Trans Roy Soc. Vol 48. (1753) pp 217-220.

106. R Price. Op cit. pp 70 and 100.

107. I Chronicles. XXI. vv 1-17.

108. e.g. H Heginbotham. *Stockport: Ancient and Modern.* (1892) p 87. and Rev J Watson. *A manuscript collection towards the History of Cheshire.* (1783). Vol 1 p 129.

109. J G Kyd (ed). Scottish Historical Society. Third Series. Vol 44. (1952).

110. R Price. Op cit. p 21 (footnote).

111. Population Studies. Vol 15. (1961-2) pp 198-200;

112. Phil Trans Roy Soc. Vol 48. (1755) pp 788-799.

113. Add MSS 4440 ff 176 et seq.

114. R Price. Op cit. p 204 (footnote).

115. William Wales. *An Inquiry into the Present State of Population in England and Wales; and the Proportion Which the present Number of Inhabitants bears to the Number at former Periods.* (1781) p 67.

116. R Price. Op cit. pp 220 and 238.

117. R Price. Op cit. p 40 (footnote).

118. J S W Gibson & M Medlycott. *Militia Lists and Musters, 1757-1876.* FFHS. 3rd ed. (1994).

119. M D Jephson. *An Anglo Irish Miscellany.* (1964).

120. Phil Trans Roy Soc. Vol 64. (1774) pp 54-66.

121. R B Wheler. *History and antiquities of Stratford upon Avon, comprising.....* (1806) pp 16-17.

122. E S Worrall. Essex Recusant. Vol 2. (1960) p 88; see also: D J Steel. *Sources for Roman Catholic and Jewish Genealogy and Family History.* NIPR. (1974) p 908.

123. R Price. Op cit. pp 35, 70, 220 and 239.

124. Hugh Calvert. *History of Hull.* (1978) p 208.

125. House of Lords Record Office. Main Papers 21 Dec 1767. [Not calendared]; see also: Catholic Ancestor. Vol 3. No 1. (Feb 1990) pp 22-26; and also: D J Steel. Op cit. pp 908-909.

126. R Price. Op cit. pp 40 (footnote), 70 and 72; see also: W Money. *History of the ancient town and borough of....Newbury, Berks....* . (1887) p 571.

127. R Price. Op cit. p 43 (footnote) for Okeford; pp 70 and 174 (footnote) for Birmingham; p 71 for Bury.

128. R Price. Op cit. pp 70 and 71.

129. ref: Swinderby par. 23/1.

130. R Price. Op cit. pp 43 (footnote) and 70.

131. F Beckwith. *The Population of Leeds during the Industrial Revolution.* Thoresby Soc. Vol 41. (1954). Miscellany. Vol 12. Pt 2. (1948) pp 118-196 and 401; see also: R Price. Op cit. pp 70 and 225 (footnote).

132. Phil Trans Roy Soc. Vol 64. (1774) pp 62-63.

133. R Price. Op cit. p 13 (footnote).

134. R Price. Op cit. p 70.

135. Phil Trans Roy Soc. Vol 64. (1774) pp 67-78. The Altrincham figures for families and inhabitants were also quoted by Price in his 'Observations' p 70; in quoting the Chester survey of houses, families and inhabitants, he states "St Michael's parish": Op cit. p 71; see also: R Price. Op cit. p 70 for Chester in 1774.

136. Phil Trans Roy Soc. Vol 68. (1778) pp 131-154.

137. R Price. Op cit. p 70 for Bolton and Little Bolton; p 23 (footnote), p 70, pp 216 and 227 (footnotes) for Manchester and Salford; p 71 for Chippenham; p 224 (footnote) for Horwick, Darwent, Cockey Moor and Chowbent; see also: Phil Tran Roy Soc. Vol 65 (1775).

138. Phil Trans Roy Soc. Vol 64. (1774) pp 438-444.

139. Phil Trans Roy Soc. Vol 68. (1778) pp 615-621.

140. T R Nash. *Collections for the history of Worcestershire.* Vol 2. (1781-1799) pp 40 and 278-279.

141. Dr W Enfield. *An Essay towards the history of Leverpool drawn up from papers left by the late Mr George Perry.* (2nd edn 1774) pp 23-24. [Price also quoted generously from Enfield's data].

142. Phil Trans Roy Soc. Vol 64. (1774) p 57; [taken from p 28 of the second edn of Enfield's 'History of Leverpool'].

143. W Boys. *Collections for a History of Sandwich in Kent, with notices of the other Cinque ports....and of Richborough.* (1792) p 832; and also: E Hasted. *History and Topographical survey of the County of Kent.* Vol 10. 2nd edn. (1801) p 379.

144. ref: PO 13.

145. R Price. Op cit. p 71. Price referred to the town as Wycombe.

146. Gentleman's Magazine. Vol 70. (1800). Pt 2 p 1160; [the information is supplied in a letter of 12 Dec 1800 where the town is referred to by its contemporary name of Chipping Wycombe].

147. R Price. Op cit p 173 (footnote).

148. Phil Trans Roy Soc. Vol 64. (1774) pp 54-66; and Vol 65. (1775) pp 322-335; see also: R Price. Op cit. pp 72 and 216 (footnote).

149. Phil Trans Roy Soc. Vol 65. (1775) pp 424-445.

150. Phil Trans Roy Soc. Vol 66. (1776) pp 160-167.

151. R Price. Op cit. pp 71 and 224/5 (footnote) for Tattenhall and Waverton and p 72 for Bala.

152. the Kilkenny listing is in the Genealogical Office, Dublin, ref: GO 443; the Waterford gentry names appear in Waterford & SE Ireland Arch & Hist Soc Journal. Vol 16 No 3 (1913).

153. R Price. Op cit. p 173 (footnote); see also: W Boys. Op cit. p 784.

154. The Irish Genealogist. Vol 5 No 1 (1974) pp 103-121; Vol 5 No 3 (1976) pp 314-334.

155. R Price. Op cit. pp 168-170.

156. R Price. Op cit. p 72 and pp 106 and 107 (footnotes).

157. T R Nash. Op cit. Vol 2 p 411.

158. R Price. Op cit. pp 166-172.

159. In Bedfordshire Family History Society Journal. Vol 6. No 3 (Autumn 1987) pp 28-32.

160. R Price. Op cit. p 71.

161. ref: Argyll Estate Papers. *List of Families residing on His Grace The Duke of Argylls Property in Kantyre (sic).... .* (1779); and *Argyll Estates Census* (1792); [in volume with Chamberlain's Accounts and Kintyre Feu Duties. Deed Box. Rosneath No 8].

162. R A Gailey. *Settlement and Population in Kintyre 1750-1800,* Scot Geog Mag. Vol 76. No II. (Sep 1960) pp 99-107.

163. R Lowe. *General View of the Agriculture of the County of Nottingham.* (2nd edn 1798). Appdx 12B pp 179-187; [1st edn was 1794]; see also: R Price. Op cit. p 70.

164. ref: D3539/1/48.

165. R Price. Op cit. pp 43 (footnote) and 70.

166. see also: T R Nash. Op cit. Vol 2. Appendix p cxvii.

167. ref: 1165 Z/Z 1.

168. ref: IR 23 (at PRO); see also: British Parliamentary Papers. (1844). HC 619. Vol 32. 389.

169. W. Wales. Op cit. p 67.

170. R Price. Op cit. p 169.

171. Main Papers 5 Mar 1781.

172. Vol 37. p 230.

173. see: D J Steel. Op cit. pp 909-910.

174. Dr J Aikin. *A description of the country from thirty to forty miles round Manchester; containing... .* (1795) p 304; R Price. Op cit. p 249 for Warrington [but on p 71 Price states this survey was made in April 1781]; R Price. Op cit. pp 71 and 175/176 (footnote) for Maidstone, 1781 and 1782.

175. R Price. Op cit. p 71 for Swindon.

176. VCH Wiltshire. Vol 8. (1965) p 93 for Warminster.

177. ref: HW 60-62.

178. R Price. Op cit. pp 204 and 205 (footnotes).

179. R Price. Op cit. pp 174 and 175 (footnotes).

180. Phil Trans Roy Soc. Vol 72. (1782) pp 35-43.

181. F M Eden. *The State of the Poor.* Vol 3. (1797) pp 750-751.

182. J Collinson. Op cit. Vol 2 pp 186 and 198.

183. F M Eden. Op cit. Vol 2 p 643.

184. H Lonsdale. *The Life of Dr Heysham.* (1780).

185. W Hutchinson. *History of Cumberland.* (1796). Vol 2 p 674.

186. Channel Islands Family History Journal. Vols 8 (Autumn 1980) - 14 (Spring 1982).

187. J Pilkington. *A View of the Present State of Derbyshire with an account of its most remarkable antiquities.* (2nd edn. 1803). Vol 2 p 338; [1st edn was 1789].

188. S Shaw. *History and antiquities of Staffordshire, compiled from....including Erdeswick's Survey... .* (1798) p 12.

189. R Lowe. Op cit. pp 172-177.

190. M Dunsford. *Historic Memoirs of the Town and Parish of Tiverton....* (1790) p 464.

191. J Hutchins. *The History and Antiquities of the County of Dorset.* (2nd edn. 1815). [1st edn was 1796]; see also: Local Population Studies. No 22. Spring 1979 pp 14-29.

192. ref: U 468.

193. Dr J Toulmin *History of Taunton in the County of Somersetshire.* (1791) pp 189-190.

194. J Toulmin *Present State of Taunton.* Monthly Magazine and British Register. Vol 17. (1804) p 528.

195. ref: Swinderby par. 23/10.

196. J Ticknell. *History of the Town and County of Kingston upon Hull.* (1796) p 854.

197. F M Eden. Op cit. Vol 3 p 827.

198. ref: DR 230/79

199. The Irish Ancestor. [Co. Leitrim] Vol 16 No 1 (1984); [Co. Waterford] Vol 8 No 1 (1976); [Co. Wexford] Vol 13 No 2 (1981).

200. F M Eden. Op cit. Vol 3 pp 750-751.

201. Journal of the Cork Historical & Archaeological Society. Vol 47, New Series. (1942).

202. The Irish Ancestor. Vol XVI. (1984).

203. J Brewster. *Parochial History and Antiquities of Stockton upon Tees....including an account....* (1829) pp 256-266.

204. C Wright. *The Brighton Ambulator, containing historical and topographical delineations of the town....* (1818) p 102.

205. Journal of the Galway Historical & Archaeological Society. Vol 9 No 1 (1978).

206. M Lloyd-Baker. *The Story of Uley.* (c1910, ND) pp 49-58; [the first edition contained neither the map nor the list of names].

207. F M Eden. Op cit. Vol 3 p 705.

208. The Irish Ancestor. Vol X No 2 (1978) pp 73-76.

209. I F W Beckett. *The Buckinghamshire Posse Comitatus, 1798.* Buckinghamshire Record Society. Vol 22. (1985); see also: British Library Stowe MSS 805 and 806.

210. J S W Gibson & M Medlycott. *Militia Lists and Musters 1757-1876.* FFHS. 3rd ed. (1994).

211. J James (ed). *Comyn's New Forest.* (1982).

212. D J Steel. *General Sources of Births, Marriages and Deaths Before 1837.* NIPR. (1976) p 336.

213. ref: MS. Top OXON c 240.

214. ref: WI/1559; the census was taken on 16 December 1833.

215. ref: P 11/28/4.

216. ref: DRO 111/46.

217. ref: 542/5/44.

Index